SCOTLAND
BLOODY SCOTLAND

for Mrs Lizzie Clark, Mid Yell
(the Centre of the Universe)

SCOTLAND BLOODY SCOTLAND

The Baron of Ravenstone

First published in 1986
by Canongate Publishing Ltd.

This edition first published in 2002
by Birlinn Ltd, West Newington House, Edinburgh,
EH9 IQS

www.birlinn.co.uk

© text and illustrations 1986
Frank Renwick of Ravenstone

British Library Cataloguing-in-Publication Data
A catalogue record for this book is available
on request from the British Library

ISBN 1 84158 221 2

Printed in Spain
by GraphyCems

PREFACE

Scotland, once a proud European nation, was sold in 1707 for £398,085 and 10 shillings. But you are probably not in Scotland to study its history. However, an understanding of that history – as distinct from the Tartan Image of the country – will certainly add to your enjoyment of this land. I have tried to include everything necessary for a proper historical framework, whilst at the same time leaving room for provocation, speculation and I hope humour. Several fuller Scottish histories are available at decent bookshops if you wish to extend your studies, as are many interesting guide books and pamphlets at the historic buildings and sites you can visit.

The Scots, for reasons you will understand if you read this book, are a people who have given up being a nation. That is the root cause of many of their problems. Do not be put off, then, if some of them you meet seem brusque, ill-mannered or ignorant of their own heritage, for these things are part of the same historical problem. To understand all is to forgive all. This slim volume with its peculiar format is designed to give the overall picture as painlessly and provokingly as possible.

Finally, if you have bought this book you have not just done yourself a favour: you have contributed to the preservation of Scotland's heritage, because all royalties accruing from its sale are going to be used to help with the restoration of a ruined Scottish castle. Thank you for your help.

Frank Renwick of Ravenstone
Baron of Ravenstone

THE BEAKER PEOPLE

The first, or earliest genuinely human, inhabitants of Scotland, then known as Alba, or White Land – so called because of the Ice Age, which totally covered it with white stuff – were the Beaker People. These simple nomadic folk had few problems or possessions. In fact, their only difficulty was in obtaining something satisfactory to put in their finely wrought Beakers to go with the ice, which they had, of course, in abundance.

Their search was to be continued by future generations and, indeed, beyond the grave, as Beaker Folk were invariably buried with their beakers, denoting religious belief in Something Better Later On. They were thus, though early, typically Scottish.

CHAMBERS

Scotland's, or Alba's, archaeological heritage commences with the Chambered Cairn. Sometimes confused with a breed of dog, the Chamber was a logical development of the Beaker, and not to be sniffed at. Various types of Cairn have been excavated, particularly at Camster, Caithness, where a most sophisticated cairn of the Type B variety may be inspected on inserting a 10p piece into the appropriate door.

Previously, these structures were erroneously thought to have been tombs, as bodies were found in some of the internal cubicles. Modern research in Edinburgh and Glasgow has however proved conclusively that bodies are still found on occasion in similar conveniences in modern times, overcome by the rigours of the climate or simply unable to unfasten the door.

CHAMBERED CAIRN, Type A.

CHAMBERED CAIRN, Type B.

CHAMBER.

STANDING STONES

Modern specialists state that these megaliths were apparently part of some vastly complicated, and fortunately long-forgotten, system for predicting the movements of heavenly bodies, and would have us believe that the sun would shine directly along the axes of these stones on Midsummer morning, or, alternatively, on Midwinter noon, were it not for the fact that the sun, and everything else in the heavens is no longer in the same relative position now as it was 10,000 years ago.

However, as the sun hardly ever appears anywhere in Scotland at these solstices – or at any other times for that matter – this interpretation may seem unnecessarily far-fetched. A more likely explanation, current in Orkney, is that they are giants turned to stone. Or possibly, as most of these megaliths are to be found in Caithness and in the Western and Northern Isles, they are the chill remains of tourists waiting for a glimpse of the sun.

BROCHS

Brochs, or Iron Age forts (*see* **A**) were built by the Picts (q.v.) and are to be found in ruinous form in many parts of Scotland, chiefly along the north and east coasts, northern isles, etc. Generations of academics have made an easy living writing learned treatises about these unique structures and how they came here in the first place.

One preposterous theory states that because the only known similar structures exist in Sardinia, the Picts were therefore Sardinian master builders who emigrated from that island. However, if this were the case, the Brochs would probably have looked more like (**B**).

Anyone with the strength to turn this page upside down can clearly see that in fact the Broch was merely a technological development of the ubiquitous Beaker.

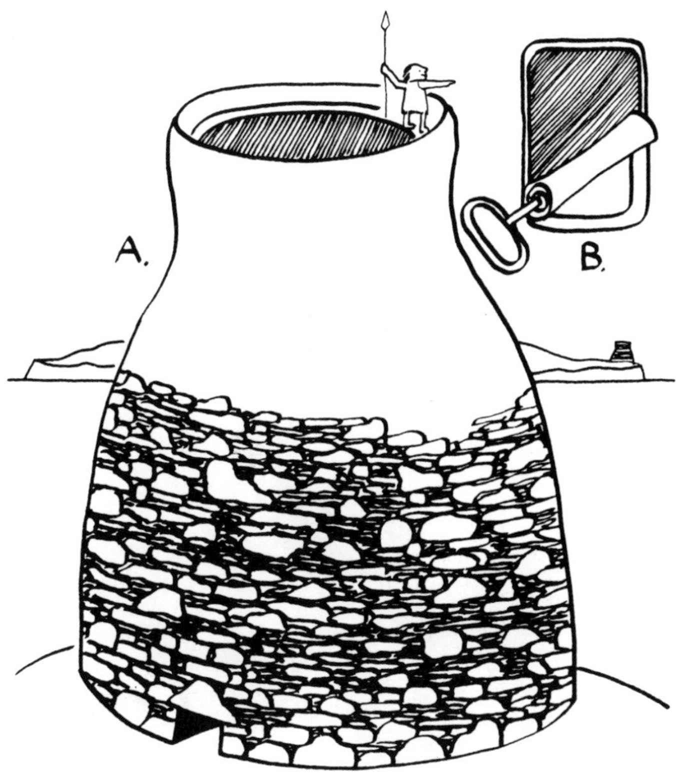

THE PICTS

The Picts were a mysterious, industrious and gifted Iron Age people, who may have come from Sardinia. They changed the name of the country, somewhat brazenly, to Pictland, covered it with Brochs, spent their spare time carving intricate patterns on stones (*see* **B**), and, according to the Romans, painting themselves (*see* **A**). To get a bit of exercise, they also fought and slew each other in complicated inter-tribal leagues and attacked the Romans as opportunity arose. That they had the resources to perfect all these skills was due in no small measure to their commercial acumen, trading with the Romans various natural products they either had no use for or had in abundance, such as bearskins, dogs (*see* Cairns), falcons and slaves.

Thus the Picts, like the Beaker Folk, contributed largely to the make-up of the classic Scot.

THE ROMANS

The Romans, whilst they did not actually conquer Scotland, made a deep and lasting contribution to the national life and character. The following incomplete list exemplifies the extent of their cultural influence: tackety boots, marching, bracing and manly pursuits and the physique that goes with them, regimental camaraderie, the kilt, civilising missions, baths, shinguards, thermal underwear, polysyllabic words, money and organised religion. The Romans, in other words, introduced middle-class values.

They changed the name of the country yet again to Caledonia, which was a lot smarter than Pictland. They are also credited with the introduction of the bagpipe, though this calumny has been hotly disputed and may indeed safely be ascribed to the vilification of later scribes to whom anything Roman was anathema.

JULIUS AGRICOLA

Agricola, Roman governor of England – then called Britain, just as nowadays Britain is generally called England – made a circumnavigation of the British Isles during his illustrious governorship, presumably as a preliminary to the proper conquest of Caledonia. He sailed as far north as to be within sight of 'Thule' – variously thought to have been Fair Isle, Foula, the Faeroe Islands or even Rockall, but now definitely located as a pub in Lerwick.

Fortunately for everyone, the Emperor Domitian wisely recalled Agricola shortly afterwards. The Romans were poor sailors.

CALGACUS, A CALEDONIAN CHIEF

Amongst the many Caledonians, or Picts, who heaved a sigh of relief at the recall of the indomitable Agricola was undoubtedly Calgacus, the Caledonian Chief, who, according to the elegant Tacitus, had led the Pictish host into the battle against Agricola's forces at the Battle of Mons Graupius, AD 84. Here, thanks to Tacitus, we encounter the first named Scotsman in history and the first Scottish battle (inauspiciously, a defeat). There is, however, some doubt about whether such an unlikely person as Calgacus ever existed, Tacitus being given to conjuring up Noble Savages purely to add substance to his ideas about politics and morality. The Picts were probably far too astute to engage in epic battles with people like the Romans. A much more plausible and more suitably named early Pictish leader was the later Run, King of the Picts.

As to the site of this illustrous battle, it would require a Heinrich Schliemann to prove the matter, and in the meantime any intelligent tourist is as likely to stumble across it as any of the covens of academics who advance various specious claims for their favourite picnic spots.

ANTONINE'S WALL

Following the departure of the masterful Agricola, the Romans reverted to a policy of safeguarding their rear, on the instigation of various gay emperors, notably Hadrian and Antonine. It is an inspiring fact that Hadrian's Wall, built all the way across England from Tyne to Solway, the biggest piece of building ever undertaken in these islands, was built to keep the Caledonians out. Antonine's Wall, stretching between Forth and Clyde, was by comparison a slightly pathetic effort, being what was then termed a *Murus Caespiticius*, or turf wall – an earthwork with a wooden palisade on top – built perhaps more as a gesture to the Picts to sod off rather than for any serious military purpose.

In summing up, we may say that the Romans undoubtedly put a lot of hard work, thought and effort into their Civilising Mission, but, like all middle class enterprises, it eventually fell to bits due to moral rot and diminishing profits. As they went down, they unleashed their ultimate deterrent, Waves of Invaders.

WAVES OF INVADERS, Part 1: THE CHURCH

Adopted by the Emperor Constantine in a moment of military euphoria, Christianity remained a secret Eastern religion, hardly ever practised, whilst the Church mushroomed into a vast international conglomerate, paying very attractive dividends to major shareholders, that not only took over the Empire but was also, by virtue of its unbridled aptitude for bigotry and venality, the main cause of its internal collapse.

Its early sales representatives in Caledonia were probably not men of the same class as had already unleashed mass religious fanaticism on Europe, but they prepared the soil on which later, more high-powered, operatives sowed and reaped. Ninian, a shadowy figure, and Columba, an escaped Irish murderer, appear to have used the same tactics as their colleagues elsewhere to subvert simple indigenous religions. Their sales pitch was successfully aimed at the chiefs and rulers, who rapidly succumbed to the obvious political advantages of the new product.

WAVES OF INVADERS, Part 2: THE SCOTS

The Caledonians, having suffered some 300 years of raids and attempted domination by the Romans, took their chance to redress the balance when the Romans left by invading and plundering the whole of Roman Britain. In this necessary work – basically a public health rather than a public relations exercise – they were aided by the Irish, who had no similar excuse, and by the Angles, Saxons and Jutes, who at least had the excuse that their own territories were sinking into the North Sea – hence causing Waves of Invaders.

The Irish, or Scots as they were then called, did not all return home, but, fancying the Mull of Kintyre and adjacent parts as a likely place for further expansion, took these from their erstwhile allies the Picts, renaming them Dalriada, after their original homeland, so proving that a Scot is at home anywhere.

FERGUS MOR MACERK

Fergus Mor, or Big Fergie, was the first real King of the Scots, having left his Irish homeland to take over the more promising Dalriada – or Dull Riada, as those better acquainted with the average rainfall in those parts have termed it.

The Scots, being Irish, were undoubtedly more set on political aggrandisement than the Picts. Dalriada spread into Argyllshire at the expense of its neighbours. Fergus's son Aedan successfully used the services of his fellow-countryman Columba to give his rule respectability and Divine Sanction (which was then very fashionable, thanks to the activities of The Church).

From the start, therefore, the Scots were acquisitive. To their eternal credit however must be placed the fact that from Ireland they brought the secret that the natives of Alba, Pictland and Caledonia had been searching for since the time of the earliest human inhabitants: what to put in the Beakers. This was the main reason the Scots were allowed to stay, and why they got away with so much in later generations.

THE VOTADINI, NOVANTAE AND DAMNONII

Not perhaps part of the normal Hong Kong Tartan image of the Scot, these Celtic or British tribes, dwelling between Hadrian's and Antonine's Walls, are very much a part of the Southern Scot's racial heritage, however unsung.

Of these, the Votadini occupied what is now Lothian and the Borders, and had two unique strongholds: Traprain Law (**A**), where the treasure came from, and Dun Eidyn – Edinburgh Castle rock. The Novantae, or Gal-Gaels, occupied Galloway and South Ayrshire, were at one time ruled by the legendary King Cole, or Coila, or Cool (**B**) – hence 'Real Cool' or Royal Cool – and had settled on crannogs (artificial lake dwellings) on account of the dampness of the climate and terrain. The aptly named Damnonii (**C**) occupied Strathclyde, for reasons best known to themselves.

WAVES OF INVADERS, Part 3: ANGLES

The Angles, or English, were Germans who, with typical teutonic guile, succeeded in passing themselves off as Angels, during the Dark Ages when there was very little light. They even managed to confuse Pope Gregory, an expert on Angels. This gave them an overwhelming superiority in a superstitious age.

Having previously conquered a large area of Roman Britain, the Angles attacked the Votadini, and, despite a spirited resistance during which the Votadini counter-attacked and got as far south as Catterick, a notorious army camp in Yorkshire, by mid seventh century the Angles were firmly established in Dun Eidyn and the whole Lothian and Borders area. Thus the whole of South-East Scotland became part of Angle-land, or England. German, later to be called Anglo Saxon, became the official language, and shortly afterwards religious bickering was introduced, chiefly over the thorny question of date-stamping Easter eggs.

These Angle territories were variously called Bernicia, Gododdin and Northumbria.

WAVES OF INVADERS, Part 4: THE VIKINGS

The Germans might possibly have looked like Angels to the Votadini, but the Vikings made them look like fairies. Scandinavians (from whom the present inhabitants of Shetland, Orkney, Caithness and to a lesser degree, the Western Isles and Sutherland claim descent) or Vikings came first as summer raiders towards the end of the eighth century and were quick to see the undeveloped potential for wholesale murder, looting, rape, arson and other forms of simple Nordic holiday fun, and stayed. Fortunately their advanced interests extended far beyond Pictland, which, sparsely populated and ill-defended, bore the brunt of their conquests in Scotland.

This lesson in what can happen when tourism gets out of hand has never been forgotten, and accounts for some of the strange behaviour modern tourists may yet encounter in the remoter regions of the land. For example, the inhabitants may take to the hills.

Whatever may have happened in the Pictish areas from the eighth century onwards, the population ceased to be Pictish and became Scandinavian. Viking raids continued till as late as the thirteenth century. Some liberal, modern historians have attempted to play down the savagery – albeit merry – of these pirates, and emphasise instead their rich cultural heritage.

KENNETH MACALPIN

In AD 843, Kenneth, King of Dalriada, in collusion with the Vikings, invaded Pictland with fire and sword, claiming their throne through his mother. For the Picts, already culturally subverted by Columba and other Irish missionaries, and constantly harassed by fifty years of Viking raids and conquests, the resulting union of the two kingdoms – now called Scotia – was The End.

Mysterious in their beginnings, the Picts' disappearance is almost as enigmatic. The culture and way of life – both of which were more pleasant and more civilised than their conquerors' – vanished. But even today in the remote Northern Isles of Shetland there are still darker-skinned, black-haired people who are demonstrably neither Vikings nor Scots in origin.

BRIEF GENEALOGY OF THE KINGS OF SCOTIA

MacAlpin, as befitted a descendant of Fergus Mor, did not sit back on his Stone Throne and enjoy his acquisitions, but continued to burn and loot his neighbours' territories in an attempt to further expand Scotia. He died on his sixth expedition into Northumbria. His demise in AD 858, was followed by 150 years of general mayhem, in which the Angles attacked the Scots and Britons (of Galloway), the Scots attacked the Angles and Britons, the Britons succeeded in expanding into Cumbria, and the Vikings attacked everyone.

Members of the Scottish royal line also indulged, in their spare moments, in continual internecine slaughter of each other, as the Succession was not by primogeniture but, in theory, by election by a group consisting of all those whose great grandfathers had held the Crown – no matter for how short a time. In practice, this meant succession by frequent parricide. A bewildering genealogy of Kenneths, Donalds, Constantines and persons with unpronounceable Irish names proliferated in rapid and obscure disorder.

CONSTITUTIONAL DEVELOPMENT

An important constitutional advance is apparent during this period of utter confusion in distinguishing between who was a true King of Scots and who were mere pretenders. The basic principal – worthy of a people that spoke and thought in Irish – was that all true Kings of Scots were distinguished by the fact that they died violent deaths, either at the hands of their enemies, their relatives or their supporters, and preferably at the hands of all three in conjunction.

This simple and self-evident constitutional principal outlived the Dark Ages, and remained basically in force right up to the End of Scotland as an independent country. The only exception was the heroic King Robert the Bruce, who had the misfortune to die of leprosy. Kings thus properly distinguished sat on The Stone Throne – a souvenir from Ireland brought over by Fergus MacErk, and invested by the clergy with spurious religious significance – until it was removed from Scone by the English King Edward, the Hammer of the Scots.

THE BRITONS GET THE CHOP

By mid-tenth century, England had become a single kingdom, and the Vikings were using Ireland as a base for their raids on the west coast. They had cleared the Britons out of Strathclyde. However, the remaining British kingdom, now confusingly called Cumbria, and comprising Galloway, Cumberland, Westmorland and parts of Lancashire, maintained a sturdy independence, though continually under attack. Its kings acknowledged the nominal suzerainty of the English king, in much the same way as their ancestors had been nominal clients of Rome.

In 937 an alliance of Scots, Vikings and Britons made an ill-conceived attempt to smash the growing power of England. This resulted in defeat at the Battle of Brunanburgh, near the Solway, and in the Scots King Constantine II doing homage to the English King Athelstane, the victor. The inaptly named Constantine thereafter retired from the political scene to a monastery.

Edmund, Athelstane's successor on the English throne, deemed it not worth the bother to be overlord of a remote and unprofitable region that was constantly under Viking attack. He transferred his suzerainty over Cumbria to the Scots King Malcolm I, who did homage to the English king for it. Thus was Galloway, and an ill-defined area of north-west England, joined to Scotia.

MALCOLM II (1005–1034), Part 1

Malcolm II, an unjustifiably obscure king, was a ruler cast in the mould of Kenneth MacAlpin and Fergus Mor. Coming to the throne in the traditional Scots way, by murdering his predecessor Kenneth III, Malcolm pursued the well-tried Scots policy of slaughtering his neighbours wherever possible, but with an added genius for profiting from their misfortunes.

In the far north, Olaf, King of Norway, a recent convert and therefore also an enthusiast for the Faith, had forcibly baptised Sigurd, Earl of Orkney, piously threatening him with death and the harrying of his earldom if he apostacised. Olaf then returned home to Norway, suitably sanctified.

Sigurd, understandably miffed, transferred his allegiance to Malcolm, who welcomed him as a brother and married him forthwith to his daughter, who, in due course, bore Thorfinn. Never one to sit around the house praying, Sigurd went off to Ireland to fight, and was soon, conveniently, slain. Thus succeeded Malcolm's grandson, Thorfinn, who thereby brought the mainland parts of the Viking earldom – Caithness, Sutherland, Ross – at least theoretically into the Scots kingdom.

MALCOLM II, Part 2

Malcolm had what many later Kings of Scots – notably the Stewarts – conspicuously lacked: luck. The first years of his reign coincided with the reign of the inept and disastrous Ethelred the Unready in England, who had to face not just the usual Viking depredations, but a wholesale war of conquest led by Cnut, a Danish king of invincible might. Malcolm was thus able to establish the classic Scots policy of profiting from English embroilment with European enemies, taking over the whole of Bernicia – Lothians and the Borders – with scarcely a blow struck in anger.

When Cnut had established himself on the English throne, he sent north an army to wrest this territory back again. The battle, at Carham on Tweed, 1018, was a glorious VICTORY FOR THE SCOTS and their allies, the Galloway Britons, led by their King, Owen the Bald.

Scotia's southern border was now fixed at the Tweed for the first time. Conveniently, Owen died that same year, and Malcolm persuaded his allies to crown his own grandson Duncan as their new king. Stretching into Lancashire on the west, mainland Scotland was now bigger than it was ever to be again.

MACBETH (1040–1057)

Malcolm's grandson Duncan I (1034–1040) succeeded him, being already King of the Cumbrians. His succession was disputed by Macbeth, Mormaer – or Earl-King – of Moray. In view of the uncertainty of the law of succession (*see* page 18) he had as good a claim as any, and probably better in the former Pictish parts of the realm.

Duncan – far from being a frail old gent murdered in his bed by Lady Macbeth – rashly invaded Morayshire to settle the matter, and did so by being slain on the battlefield. Macbeth therefore became king in the accepted and undisputable manner, by slaying his predecessor.

Macbeth seems to have been rather jollier than your average Scots Dark Ages King – probably because he was Pictish – and was the first to go abroad on holiday, or pilgrimage as it was then called. He visited Rome, where, as chroniclers tell us, he 'scattered money among the poor like seed'. Whose money it was is not recorded, but it certainly was not Scots money, as that was not yet invented.

LULACH THE SIMPLE (1057–1058)

Macbeth's successful rebellion was part of Pictish dissatisfaction with the increasing domination of southern, particularly Angle, interests over the whole of Scotia. Like all successful Scottish businesses, the House of Alpin, under the managing directorship of sharp practitioners like Malcolm II, was almost obsessed with expansion into English markets. This Scots death-wish – that the Big Time is always south of the Border – was anathema to the Pictish-descended inhabitants, to whom, since Roman times, anything from south of Antonine's Wall was to be resisted to the death. In this folk wisdom, the Pict population again demonstrated their superior intelligence over the Scots, but to little avail.

In 1054, Duncan's son Malcolm invaded Macbeth's kingdom with an English army, driving Macbeth out of Lothian and later slaying him in 1057. Even then, with Malcolm's forces in their home territory, the Moray Picts chose Macbeth's stepson, Lulach the Simple, to be their king. After a dodgy seven months reign, this unfortunate was slain by Malcolm. However, by dying in this acceptable and time-honoured fashion, Lulach was at least a proven True King of Scots.

MALCOLM III, or CANMORE (1058–1093)

Having gained the throne with English military support, Malcolm repaid his benefactor, the saintly Edward the Confessor, at whose court he had experienced many years of hospitality, by burning, raiding and looting the north of England, a policy he continued throughout his reign.

In 1066, however, the English ceased to run their own show, and were taken over by William I and the Normans. Shortly thereafter, by an extraordinary quirk of fate, the Saxon royal family were picked up by a passing sailor on the beach at Rosyth. Among them was the Princess Margaret, whom Malcolm swiftly took as his second wife. Fancying he now had a claim to the whole of England – hence the nickname Canmore, or Big Head – Malcolm prepared another foray against the luckless Northumbrians, little anticipating what was to follow.

A massive invasion by William's army of hauberk-clad knights and its support fleet offshore forced Malcolm to retreat with his tribal levies farther and farther into his own kingdom until, cornered at Abernethy, in Perthshire, he chose to swear fealty to William rather than certain destruction (1072). He and his kingdom were hopelessly outclassed.

In 1092, Malcolm lost Cumbria south of the Solway to William II, before being murdered at Alnwick.

QUEEN MARGARET or SAINT MARGARET

Malcolm III's English wife, later known as Saint Margaret – patron saint of White Settlers – was definitely a cut above the usual Gruochs, Ingibjorgs, etc., that had normally sported the consort's diadem.

Thwarted by Fate's Decree (*see* page 25) in her ambition to become a nun, she had an indomitable will to civilise (i.e. Anglicise) everything she came into contact with in her rude matrimonial kingdom, starting with the language, which, in court circles, henceforth became English (or, more correctly, Northumbrian). Totally without humour – according to her chaplain, she 'never laughed' – she was tirelessly religious, interfered incessantly in the church, stamping out native abuses and customs and substituting more up-to-date ones. She also founded Dunfermline Abbey, close by Malcolm's palace, where she introduced pomp and display, costly raiment, tapestries, gold and silver plate, spices and foreign drink. Flemish and Dutch merchants took up residence in Fife to purvey such items, paying a mulct to the royal treasury for the privilege.

DONALD II, DUNCAN II and DONALD II (again)

The Picts and Scots of the north seethed with discontent against the rapid advance of Anglicisation and all that came with it, particularly no doubt, the foreign drink. With Malcolm dead in England and Margaret dying in Edinburgh, Donald Bain, Malcolm's brother – who by Celtic tradition had the best claim – seized the throne with northern support for a programme of rapid de-Anglicisation.

William II, however, was determined to keep Scotland a vassal state under Anglo-Norman influence, and he provided an army to support a rival claimant, Duncan II, Malcolm's son by his first wife and a longtime resident in England.

When Duncan's brief reign (mid-1094) was terminated in time-honoured fashion by Donald and his Celtic army, William provided more Anglo-Normans to place Edgar, son of Malcolm and Margaret, on the throne. As a generous gesture to the new civilisation, the captive Donald was not slain, but blinded and locked away for life. Despite this, however, he still counts as a True King, the last in fact, of the Celtic House of Alpin.

EDGAR (1097–1107)

The House of Canmore – that is, the descendants of Malcolm III and Margaret – started with Edgar, and went on till 1286. Primogeniture replaced the previous, rough, Picto-Scottish system of inheritance, although from time to time claimants from the north with rights under that system still appeared.

It had been obvious from the first day of William the Conqueror's advance into Scotland that the old tribal levies were no match for Norman feudal warfare, and William Rufus had reinforced the message. It was equally plain to the House of Canmore that feudal monarchy and close relations with England were passports out of the mountains and moors and into the Big League.

Edgar, a bachelor, remained at peace with his overlords throughout his reign. He removed his capital to Edinburgh Castle, and had little interest in anything north of the Forth. When Magnus Barelegs, King of Norway, threatened to invade the west, Edgar bought him off, acknowledging Magnus as King of the Western Isles. He was even prepared to stretch his definition of an island to include the Kintyre peninsula – the very springboard from which Fergus Mor had founded the Scottish kingdom.

ALEXANDER I (1107–1124)

The Norman kings of England, having clearly established the fact that Scotland was a vassal state, turned their attention elsewhere, and a long period of unaccustomed peace ensued between the two nations, broken only by occasional rash adventures of Scots kings into England.

Alexander, who succeeded his brother Edgar, had, like him, spent years at the English court learning Norman ways. He married an illegitimate daughter of his overlord Henry I, and served him on his Welsh campaign in 1114. Norman knights and younger sons flocked northwards in increasing numbers to receive feudal baronies from Alexander in southern Scotland, and to build the first motte and bailey castles. (A nice surviving motte can be seen at Mochrum, Galloway.)

The rude inhabitants, who had previously regarded their chiefs as tribal paternalists, now became peasants overnight, forced to labour at castle building and accountable for their lives to Pit and Gallows, their courts presided over as often as not by total foreigners.

DAVID I (1124–1153)

King David, the third son of Malcolm and Margaret to wear the crown, succeeded Alexander, who had died without legitimate issue. David was then over forty, had spent much of his life at the English court and on the manors of his English wife, Matilda. As an heiress, she had brought him the Earldom of Northampton and the manor of Huntingdon. He was thus, to all intents and purposes, an Anglo-Norman aristocrat, as were his friends and all his officials of state and church. The Anglo-Norman takeover of Scotland, initiated by his two predecessors, became an establishment in which land tenure and a man's position in its hierarchy replaced the ancient bond of kin and clan. The Highlands, and for the time being, Galloway, were not party to this uncalled-for intrusion. The Normans had conquered England in a fair fight: they conquered Scotland at the invitation of her kings.

The House of Canmore, however, was better at conquering its own subjects than defeating external enemies. In 1138, David attempted to profit from the Stephen *v.* Matilda conflict in England by invading the north of that country, where at the Battle of the Standard, he was defeated by a geriatric archbishop. The Gallowegians in the Scots army fought like demons, whilst most of the new feudal nobles changed sides half-way through the battle.

THE CHURCH

All the kings of the House of Canmore were keen on The Church – as was indeed fitting for a feudal aristocracy. Like their Foundress and Patron, St Margaret, they in their turn founded and richly endowed huge cathedrals and monasteries, and in this they were emulated by many of their nobles. David I was later termed 'A sair Sanct for the Croun' on account of his lavish benefactions, involving the alienation of vast tracts of crown land. They packed these institutions full of outlandish orders of foreign monks, canons, friars, pardoners, etc., most of them living in comparative luxury on the tithes of the peasantry and the proceeds of their lands.

It is true that by their industry, some of these entrepreneurs advanced agriculture, helped cure rich people, provided sanitary accommodation for travellers of the right class, and employed considerable numbers of the common folk one way or another on menial tasks. They also performed certain religious ceremonies – separated from the grubby populace behind richly carved screens – whose principal object was to keep people in awe and in their place.

The old Scottish independent monk-priests, called Culdees, that had evolved in the Dark Ages – and who had developed certain undesirable tendencies like marrying and living like ordinary folk – were finally tidied away and replaced by pukka, hierarchy-approved, operatives.

BURGHS

Towns did not exist in Scotland in pre-Canmore times, nor did money. What trade existed was simple barter, and needs were few. Needs now multiplied, and provision had to be made to make it possible for merchants – that is, foreign merchants – to cater for the new society in relative security. David I and his successors issued charters establishing Royal Burghs which, advertised through the media of the churches, set out the conditions and duties, rewards and payments for would-be burghers. Barons followed suit with Burghs of Barony.

It cannot be denied that the conditions were relatively attractive, nor that the burghs – and to a lesser extent the castles and ecclesiastical foundations – provided important opportunities for long undeveloped native talents. For the first time, folk with marketable skills could make a living other than on the land or in some war-band. The royal treasury lived off the proceeds in rents, tolls, tax and duties.

MALCOLM THE MAIDEN (1153–1165)

King David's son, Prince Henry, predeceased him, so that when David died his grandson, Malcolm IV, aged eleven, succeeded. Malcolm, who did homage to his overlord Henry II at Chester in 1157, continued the Canmore policy of conquering his own subjects with the help of Anglo-Norman soldiery, and extended the power of the feudal baronage north of the Forth and Clyde. An English chronicler wrote: 'Recent kings of Scotland profess themselves to be rather Frenchmen, both in race and manners, language and culture; and, after reducing the Scots to utter servitude, they admit only Frenchmen to their friendship and service.'

Malcolm is said to have subjugated the Gallowegians – which means he turned loose his baronial foreigners among them – though this was later reversed by the doughty Gallgaels. In Argyll, the Scots chose Somerled, a leader who had more in common with Fergus Mor than Malcolm, to drive out the Vikings. Their continuing inroads had gone unchecked since the reign of Edgar. They then spent twelve years happily laying waste the new burgh of Glasgow, its vicinity and cathedral, until Somerled's defeat and death.

Malcolm, like Edgar, died unmarried.

WILLIAM THE LION (1165–1214)

Malcolm IV may or may not have been a maiden, but his brother who succeeded him was certainly no lion. He it was, however, who chose this martial beast for his escutcheon, and it has remained on the Royal Arms of Scotland ever since.

Wishing to play the knight errant in the Big League, William revived the hoary Scottish claim to Northumbria whilst Henry II was having little local difficulties with his sons and Thomas Becket. William's invasion of the north of England was considerably more disastrous than his grandfather's had been. He was captured at Alnwick, and, with his feet tied under his horse's belly, he travelled through England to the jeers of the populace and the merry ringing of church bells.

His overlord treated him exactly as he would have treated any other of his many vassals: harshly and with contempt. The Lion was shipped to Normandy and caged in Falaise Castle from where he was eventually released after handing over Edinburgh and Stirling Castles and three Border fortresses to English garrisons, and swearing fealty, along with all his barons, for all their lands.

In 1189, in return for 10,000 marks paid into the crusading fund of Richard I, this Treaty of Falaise was rescinded, but the Lion never ventured forth again, except to oppress his own subjects.

ALEXANDER II (1214–1249)

By the thirteenth century, it was plain that Scotland was going to remain feudal, governed by a king and baronage that were almost entirely Anglo-Norman either by descent or by emulation. Humans, as every Scot – as distinct from every Pict – knows, must evolve or go under. The advantage now lay clearly with the Canmore principle: If you can't beat them, join them. Canmore rule and policy, though it cannot escape the taint of the Quisling, had resulted in some very positive advantages – achieved at the cost of servitude.

Thus, in Alexander's reign, when he launched final campaigns to subjugate traditional areas of resistance, he was aided by Celtic chiefs as much as by English soldiers. The wild Gallowegians, free descendants of the Britons, were finally conquered and feudalised, although, even as late as 1384, Galloway retained its own laws. In Moray, that seat of Macbeth's successful Celtic rebellion, a continuing series of risings led by descendants of Duncan II was ended brutally. At Halkirk, in Caithness, where the Church was as yet almost the sole representer of Anglo-Norman rule, a bishop was boiled in butter by the parishioners who objected to his financial exactions. Ninety suspects had their hands and feet hacked off. In the west, Alexander reconquered Argyll from the descendants of Somerled, but a seaborne mission to regain the Western Isles ended when the King died prematurely on the journey.

HOO LANG, WID YE SAY NOO, CHESSAG, TIL DEEP-FRY A BISHAP?

ALEXANDER III (1249–1286), Part 1

The reign of Alexander III, the last king of the House of Canmore, was, at least in retrospect, a Golden Age. Later generations looked back to it as a time of unimaginable felicity because the country over which Alexander ruled was at peace with itself and with England, and because there was strong central government, ably served and personally supervised by the King. A network of roads, ferries and bridges linked over fifty Royal Burghs, in which merchants and craftsmen pursued their trades free from baronial interference and depredation. Big business – that is, The Church – was thriving in agriculture, the salt and coal trade, estate management and property development.

Of course, beyond the Highland Line, the unconquered Gaelic population still lived largely outwith this society, and the soldier on the ramparts of Sirling Castle looked north onto a virtually unknown and impenetrable Caledonia, much as Hadrian's legionaries had done a thousand years before. Alexander's victory at Largs, 1263, over a large and final Viking invasion led by Haakon, King of Norway, led to the handing over of sovereignty over the Western Isles. But the Islesmen and their fellow Gaels and Norse Gaels throughout the far north-west Highlands cared no more about the so-called King of Scots than they had about the Kings of Norway. To them, the Kings of Scots were total aliens.

ALEXANDER III, Part 2

Alexander's reign, albeit a Golden Age by comparison with what followed, was in its early years uncannily flavoured with some of the not-so-Golden features that were to become commonplace in the 'Dark and Drublie Days' ahead. The King succeeded as a minor, aged eight, and two baronial factions contended for control. When he was ten, he was married to Margaret, daughter of Henry III of England, and Henry thereafter began to build up one of the factions as a pro-English party, ostensibly to secure proper treatment for his little daughter. The opposing faction thus became an anti-English one – whether for patriotic reasons, as optimistic historians aver, or because they didn't receive English bribes – and the two Royal children were alternately seized and liberated as the factions struggled for power. This situation ended when Alexander came of age, and his relations with Edward I, his brother-in-law, were perfectly amicable.

Alexander died a famous death, when his horse fell from a cliff-top near Kinghorn, in Fife.

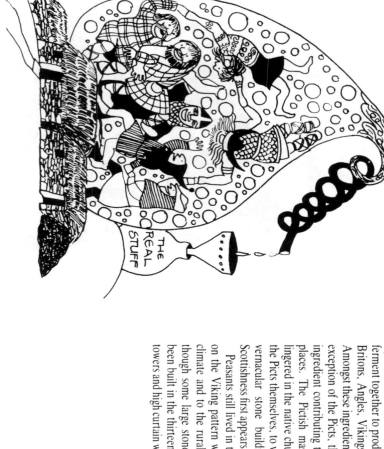

THE CULTURAL MIX

By the end of the thirteenth century, all the basic ingredients that were to ferment together to produce the modern Scot were in the pot: Picts, Irish, Britons, Angles, Vikings, Normans and a dash of Flemings and Dutch. Amongst these ingredients, the Normans were the yeast. With the notable exception of the Picts, there was then no Scottish culture as such. Each ingredient contributing to the heady mixture was derivative from other places. The Pictish mastery of building and stoneworking, that had lingered in the native church until that too was feudalised, appeared, like the Picts themselves, to vanish mysteriously. Yet it is in the emergence of vernacular stone buildings in the following centuries that a real Scottishness first appears.

Peasants still lived in turf hovels but in the far north stone longhouses on the Viking pattern were abuilding. These were well adapted to the climate and to the rural necessities. Castles were still mainly wooden, though some large stone ones, such as Dirleton and Kildrummie, had been built in the thirteenth century Anglo-Norman fashion, with circular towers and high curtain walls.

THE CULTURAL MIX *continued*

True Scottish castles, the small and fantastically varied peels or tower houses of the minor feudal barons and lairds, had yet to evolve. It was only when the comparative peace and order of Canmore times crumbled away into a welter of endless rebellions and widespread lawlessness that castle building became a national art form, a true expression of a very turbulent, vigorous and uncouth people. These later castles covered the country in thousands.

The only other popular, secular art form of medieval Scotland was its heraldry – again, at this time, still only a derivative. Yet in the course of the following turbulent centuries, it became, like castle building, much more broadly and popularly applied, and far less elitist, than elsewhere. By 1707, according to the late Sir Thomas Innes of Learney, Lord Lyon King of Arms, one in every forty-five Scots was of – or directly related to someone of – noble birth. Coats of Arms were everywhere, and had, therefore, a wider significance and appeal than tartan.

THE CULTURAL MIX *concluded*

Nowadays, visitors to such Scottish castles that have not been turned into stately homes assume that their internal walls were originally as they are now, bare stonework. In fact, they were originally painted with rich, bright heraldry, or covered with similarly emblazoned tapestries. The painting, like the building, was done mainly by local craftsmen, and their talents would often thereafter have been employed on humbler dwellings. Church windows also sparkled with the heraldry of benefactors – most of it later destroyed in bloody wars and reformations. In the burghs, burghers and their guilds proclaimed their callings in similar fashion. Clothes, banners, seals, plate, were all heraldic, combining a bright and fascinating display in primary colours with an ancient Scots passion for tracing kinship. Heraldry was the pop art of medieval Scotland.

The nobles themselves, like their art, were strictly functional, as essential a group to the functioning of the realm as hewers of wood and drawers of water. There were Earls – the only noble title to predate the Normans – and Barons, holding their lands *in liberam baroniam* of the King, entitled in their leisure moments to wear the scarlet Cap of Maintenance, signifying their right to exercise jurisdiction in their own mini-kingdoms. A variety of gilt coronets later sprang out around this simple headpiece, but it remains to this day the badge of the Scots feudal barony.

THE MAID OF NORWAY (1286–1290)

Although he had recently remarried, all Alexander's children, and his English wife, sister of Edward I, had predeceased him. The heiress to the throne was Margaret, a three-year-old Norwegian princess, daughter of King Eric II who had married Alexander's daughter.

The earls and barons, bishops and abbots chose six Guardians of the realm to govern in her name until arrangements could be made to bring her to Scotland. They sent to Edward as their overlord, as they were in feudal duty bound to do, for advice and assistance.

The danger lay in baronial claimants using the sudden removal of the Royal power to advance their various claims to the succession. Bruce, Lord of Annandale, did so directly. News of the unrest reached Eric in Norway, and he became even more reluctant to part with his little daughter. In 1290, however, he agreed with Edward to send Margaret to England, where she was to be betrothed to Edward's infant son.

The little Princess died on the way there, in Orkney, whether from shipwreck, sea-sickness or home-sickness is unknown. She never set foot in her Kingdom, and her little body returned home to be buried in Bergen.

THE THIRTEEN CLAIMANTS (1290–1292)

It is true to say that the death of Alexander III was the unluckiest event ever to happen in Scotland. But now, after 200 years of forcibly introducing a foreign system, foreign nobles, foreign prelates, doing homage regularly to the Kings of England and resolutely setting their faces against their own people and heritage, the legacy of the House of Canmore came home to roost.

Thirteen contenders for the throne, most of them with powerful feudal support but none with enough power to overawe the rest, sprang like mushrooms from various defunct branches of the Royal tree. The Guardians summoned Edward to judge between them, which he painstakingly did, after spending over a year listening to their lengthy and tortuous depositions, by the Award of Norham (November, 1292). All the claimants had previously sworn fealty to Edward, and the chosen one, John Balliol, swore fealty again on becoming King.

It is impossible to fault Edward for carrying out his feudal duties as acknowledged overlord of Scotland, and his choice cannot really be faulted either, in its adherence to feudal law. He would have been less than astute if, at the same time, he had not taken the opportunity of making his own position as overlord perfectly clear.

KING JOHN BALLIOL (1292–1296)

Edward had spent ten years conquering Wales, and was engaged in conquering and defending choice portions of France. His attitude to Scotland was perfectly straightforward: Scotland was – and had been at least since the time of William the Conqueror – a vassal state. His feudal duty was to maintain law and order there. When Balliol proved incompetent, derided as a 'Toom Tabard', or English stooge, by jealous and thwarted rivals, and when a council of these concluded an alliance with the King of France, Edward returned to Scotland in March, 1296, with an army, to prevent the situation deteriorating.

Two aspects of Canmore feudalism ensured that he would be unopposed: (1) Apart from subjugating the natives, and one or two disastrous forays into the north of England, the Scots knew nothing about warfare; and (2) Almost all the Scots barons also held fiefs in England which would be forfeit if they took up arms against the English King.

In fact the only real resistance to the invasion was provided by thirty Flemish merchants at Berwick, who fought to the death in their own burning hall. At Roxburgh, the castle surrendered as soon as the English asked for it, and at Stirling, the garrison fled when the English approached. Balliol surrendered the kingdom to Edward at Brechin, whereupon Edward, after making a leisurely journey to Elgin to see the sights, returned to England with Balliol, the ancient Stone Throne (*see* page 19) and other souvenirs.

It had taken him ten years hard fighting to subdue the Britons in Wales, but only five months to conquer feudal Scotland.

HOW FLORENTINE CAPITALISTS SAVED SCOTLAND

ER, IT'S ABOUT THE KING OF ENGLAND'S SCOTS INVASION, GENTLEMEN...

Militarily, 200 years of increasing feudalism had left Scotland no better off than when Malcolm Canmore had faced William I at Abernethy (*see* page 25): they were still hopelessly outclassed. As for the English, at no time had they wished to conquer Scotland. Their interests lay elsewhere, in France.

Now, however, that had perforce changed. If Scotland was not going to be governed by a Scots King – as Balliol's reign had apparently shown – and if, as well as being a hotbed of disorder it was to be even more troublesome by active alliance with France, then it was plainly Edward's duty to his own country to subjugate it permanently, as he had done with Wales. Edward was never a king to shirk his duty.

That he did not ultimately succeed was due in large part to overstretched finances. He was already heavily in debt to Florentine moneylenders to pay off his Welsh campaigns and massive castle building programme there. In Scotland therefore for financial reasons, he had to confine himself to building castles which, like Antonine's Wall, were of wood and earth. The English, like the Romans, could not really afford to conquer Scotland.

SIR WILLIAM WALLACE

In 1296, the Kingdom of Scotland ceased to exist and became like Wales, a remote and undesirable part of the Kingdom of England. Edward despised the place, because of the pusillanimous way it had given in, and he hated it because of the threat it posed to his French ambitions. The English soldiers, judges, tax collectors and nobles who now governed the land shared their King's opinions, and acted accordingly: with contempt, and harshly.

But the Scots were, in those days, a perverse people. They would thole any amount of contemptuous treatment from their own rulers, however tenuously Scottish, but when the English tried it (especially the taxation) they raised more Scottish national feeling in a few months than the Canmores had done in two centuries.

Sir William Wallace was an unknown Lanarkshire knight. Fighting in the name of the discredited Balliol, he headed a rapidly mounting resistance along with de Moray in the north. This was mainly composed of people of little or no feudal account, and from the traditional areas of British, Pictish and Gaelic resistance: Strathclyde, Galloway and the north. The nobles, with more to lose, skulked at home, except for bold self-seekers like Bruce, Earl of Carrick – grandson of Bruce, Lord of Annandale, who was one of the Thirteen Claimants (*see* pages 41–42) – who changed sides frequently, posing now as a patriot, now as Edward's ally.

THE BATTLE OF STIRLING BRIDGE (11 September 1297)

de Cressingham
(A) BEFORE,
+ (B) AFTER:
IT'S A WEE GIFTIE FRAE STIRLING BRIDGE, SON.

King Edward was now in France, where he enjoyed being best. The Governor of Scotland was the somewhat geriatric, and usually absentee, de Warenne, Earl of Surrey. The real power was wielded by Hugh de Cressingham, a fat, conceited, ambitious Churchman, who, like many of that ilk, delighted in playing the soldier and slaughtering his fellow men. He was not the most popular Englishman to rule over Scotland, although several modern Secretaries of State have been fully as obnoxious.

With castle after castle falling to the Scots resistance armies north of the Forth, the English army advanced to Stirling Bridge, where, inconceivably, and due at least in part to conflicting orders from de Warenne and de Cressingham, it was cut to pieces by the wild Scots rabble, with their little shields, scant armour, dirks and Lochaber axes. It was the first time ever that the Scots had defeated an English feudal army – and that without any help from the Scottish nobility, except for the Earl of Lennox, and James, the High Steward.

To celebrate, the dead, bloated body of de Cressingham – left on the field whilst de Warenne beat it to Berwick – was cut up into little bits and sent to friends and relatives all over the country as a 'Wee Giftie' – the birth of the Scottish souvenir industry.

With the death from wounds of his ally de Moray, Wallace was now Guardian of Scotland, but in the name of an Empty-Coat King. The nobles disdained support. If only Wallace had declared a Scots Republic!

But in January 1298, the French, not for the last time, reneged on the terms of their alliance with the Scots by concluding a separate peace with Edward.

THE DEATH OF WALLACE, 1304

Freed by the French truce from his embroilments in that country, Edward returned to England, spent the winter preparing his response to his northern rebels, and in July 1298 inflicted a crushing defeat on Wallace's Peoples Army at Falkirk. The tightly packed schiltroms, or 'hedgehogs', of Scots spearmen, deserted by their feudal cavalry, could not hold out against the heavily armed English knights and superb Welsh longbowmen.

Wallace, a heroic figure without equal in the history of his country, took to the hills and moors again with his bands, and was at one time in Europe attempting to gain foreign support. In May 1304, he was betrayed by a Scots knight, taken to England, tried, and given the traditional execution of the traitor: drawn and hanged, beheaded, disembowled, his entrails burnt, his head exposed on London Bridge, his right arm on the bridge at Newcastle and his left at Aberdeen.

Wallace would have been the first to admit that he and his compatriots were just as brutal (his sword belt was tastefully covered with de Cressingham's skin), yet the justice of his cause and of his words at his cursory trial has echoed long after him: 'I am not a traitor to Edward, as Edward is not my King.'

THE DEATH OF EDWARD, 1307

In September 1305, with Edward's forces firmly in control of Scotland south of the Forth, ten Scots and twelve English commissioners drew up at Westminster an Ordinance for the Governing of Scotland. It guaranteed the Scots their traditional rights, laws and freedoms as in the time of Alexander III, except that their king was to be the King of England. It was, in the circumstances, a forbearing and statesmanlike document, and virtually the whole Scots feudal establishment accepted it.

Edward, 'The Hammer of the Scots', was now sixty-six, and the Ordinance reflects a sober and magnanimous desire for peace. He had done his duty as overlord of Scotland and as King of England, and the settlement was in no sense an attempt at forced Anglicisation. Much the same settlement, in fact, prevailed after 1603.

But, like his arch-enemy Wallace, Edward was a man born before his time, and a man, therefore, doomed in the end to fail. A few months later, Bruce irrevocably rebelled. It was to crush this rebellion that Edward, worn out and ill, journeyed north in 1307, and died on the Border.

DEATH OF THE RED COMYN, 1306

Robert de Brus, Scotticé Bruce, Earl of Carrick, was a self-seeking feudal adventurer with a claim to the defunct Scottish throne. He appears to have combined in his character the driving ambition and opportunism of a feudal noble and the blood-thirsty savagery of the pre-Canmore Scot, though only a few drops of his blood were actually Scottish. During Edward's reign, he changed sides frequently. He had served as commander of the English garrison at Ayr, and had supplied siege engines to the English for their assault on Wallace's fellow rebels at Stirling Castle. He was in no sense a patriot in the Wallace mould.

Gradually, with considerable cunning, Bruce had built up support without ever fully showing his ambition. But a powerful rival claimant, John Comyn of Badenoch, stood in his way. Early in 1306, in the church of the Grey Friars, Dumfries, Bruce and Comyn met at Bruce's request to see if they could patch up their differences. When Comyn proved obdurate, Bruce, in a passion, knifed him down, and his followers finished him off.

In March, Bruce had himself crowned at Scone (the traditional crowning place of the Scots kings, where the ancient Stone Throne had rested before Edward had taken it to England where it still remains, under the throne at Westminster Abbey), but the prospects looked very bleak. Comyn had had many powerful kinsmen and friends, ranging in area from Buchan in the north, through Argyll and into Galloway. These, like the English, were implacably opposed to Bruce. The Church, which had for ecclesiastical reasons hoped to support him, was forced to excommunicate him for slaying Comyn on hallowed ground.

ROBERT ON THE RUN

While Edward I lived, Bruce's crown wasn't worth the paper it was written on. Few men of any standing felt like chucking away their chances by siding with an excommunicated murderer and notorious oath-breaker. Defeated at Methven by Aymer de Valence, Edward's new commander in Scotland, and at Dalry by John of Lorne, a Comyn kinsman, the self-made king fled from his kingdom, leaving his wife and younger brother Nigel at Kildrummie Castle. Later his wife, sisters and daughter were dragged from sanctuary at Tain. His supporters were rounded up and either imprisoned, or, like Nigel Bruce, hanged.

Bruce returned to Scotland in February 1307, some say from Norway, some from Ulster. His brothers Alexander and Thomas landed in Galloway with a small Irish force, and were defeated and executed by the MacDowalls, a powerful Galloway clan, kinsmen of Comyn and Alexander of Argyll.

Bruce's fortunes were then at their lowest ebb. He lived as a hunted outlaw with only a handful of companions in the remote Galloway hills. But Bruce had what few Scottish kings after him had for long: luck. It was just at this time (1307) that Edward died.

EDWARD II

Alexander had been succeeded by a young girl: Edward I was succeeded by Edward II. From that moment on, it became gallingly obvious to Scots barons and English garrisons alike that they were on their own. The new King of England did have his interests, but his feudal responsibility in Scotland was not one of them. His old father's dying wish had been to have his flesh boiled off his bones, and these bones borne in a leather bag at the head of his army in Scotland. This was precipitately abandoned as the new monarch headed back to the gay life in London.

Seldom in British history has a pretender had such a stroke of luck as Bruce. His cause turned overnight into a triumph that gained rapidly increasing baronial backing from such barons as now decided to remain in Scotland and forfeit their English manors. Other baronial families, seeing the way things were likely to go and choosing the opposite course, now disappear from Scottish history.

BRUCE ON THE WARPATH

Bruce was not slow to seize his advantage. In a winter campaign, 1307–1308, he wasted the Comyn stronghold, the Earldom of Buchan, with fire and sword. During the following winter, he routed John of Lorne and Alexander of Argyll out of the land. His brother, Edward Bruce, waged similar destruction meanwhile against the MacDowalls in Galloway. With every success, more men flocked to join them: it was wise to make friends with such a man as Bruce.

Next, having thus smashed the domestic opposition, Bruce turned his attention to the English garrisons. The wood and earth castles that Edward had erected for want of finance (*see* page 44) were soon taken and razed. The pre-Edwardian stone castles, which Edward had in many cases elaborated, had to be taken by subterfuge or starvation, as the Scots lacked expensive siege machines. Many are the legends of pluck and daring that tell of Bruce's lieutenants such as Douglas and Randolph, taking huge castles like Edinburgh and Roxburgh. At Roxburgh – outside Kelso – whilst the English and their pals held Shrovetide revelry, Douglas and his men sneaked up on them disguised as cows. By summer 1314, Stirling Castle alone remained in English hands.

Nor were Bruce's activities now confined to his own kingdom. Much to his subjects' pleasure and profit, that traditional sport of true Scots Kings, raiding into northern England, was revived on a regular basis, the English as far south as Richmond paying an annual geld to Bruce to be spared his attentions.

Norman he may have been, French he certainly spoke, murderer and excommunicate he definitely was, but Bruce was the sort of man that Scots warm to.

THE BATTLE OF BANNOCKBURN, 1314

This major battle, the only one ever fought by Bruce, arose out of a chivalrous agreement between Edward Bruce and de Mowbray, the English Governor of Stirling Castle, to wit, that if by Midsummer Day, 1314, the King of England had not brought an army to relieve Stirling, then it should be handed over without further delay or bloodshed to the besieging Scots.

Both Bruce and the English king had cause to wish that this agreement had never been arrived at. Already wildly unpopular with his own barons, Edward was forced to come to Scotland and fight. It committed Bruce to stopping a full-scale English army, something the Scots were totally ill-equipped to do. All his many successes to date had been skirmishes and guerrilla actions: everyone remembered what had happened to Wallace at Falkirk. Barring an unforeseen organisational blunder, as at Stirling Bridge, or a major tactical mistake, there was no way the Scots could defeat an army pre-eminent in Europe for its discipline, cavalry and longbowmen.

On 23 June, 7,000 lightly armed Scots faced 20,000 English troops at Bannockburn, outside Stirling. Bruce's luck did not desert him. During the night, the English changed their position, and Bruce, seeing this in amazement on Midsummer morning, realised at once that he had what he most needed – a major tactical blunder. No one knows now why Edward had moved his mighty force into a confined area of marshland, but Bruce exploited the error to the full. Both armies fought magnificently all day, but it ended at last in a bloody and disastrous rout of the English. Edward was lucky to escape to Dunbar.

KING ROBERT THE BRUCE

Bruce was now unquestionably *de facto* King of Scots. A parliament at Cambuskenneth Abbey passed sentence of forfeiture on all who did not now do homage. Vast amounts of spoil and ransoms for captured English barons and knights helped fill many a Scots purse and sporran. Wallace's rising had been sparked off by taxation. De Cressingham had been especially hated because he was Treasurer (or Chancellor of the Exchequer). Patriotism may or may not have been a strong force in the struggle, but finance certainly was.

Bruce's two staunchest supporters throughout his struggle, Thomas Randolph, Earl of Moray, and Lord James Douglas, now became his principal councillors. Records are few of the legislation enacted during the rest of Bruce's reign, though what exists shows a determined effort to restore law and order.

In England, the misguided Edward blundered from one crisis to another and was forced to abdicate in 1327. His wife Isabella and her lover, Mortimer, took over the government. They went bankrupt, couldn't pay their forces, and were forced by Scots invasions to sign the Treaty of Edinburgh, acknowledging Bruce to be King of Scots. All English claims to sovereignty over Scotland were renounced and arrangements were made for David, Bruce's infant son, to marry Joan, Edward III's sister.

THE DECLARATION OF ARBROATH, 1320

The Churchmen of Scotland had generally been supporters of Bruce, chiefly due to an interminable ecclesiastical quarrel as to whether or not Scotland was subject to the Archbishop of York. They had long since absolved themselves from observing their Pontiff's excommunication of Bruce. It remained in force officially, however, and Bruce could not be accepted internationally so long as His Holiness withheld recognition.

The Declaration, sent to Pope John XXII in 1320 by eight earls and thirty-one barons was drawn up by Bernard de Linton, Abbot of Arbroath, Chancellor of Scotland, and a wordsmith of some considerable acuity. It makes a very fair statement of Scotland's treatment at the hands of Edward I, and of how Robert had delivered the Kingdom. Fancifully, it declares that the assembled nobility had fought 'not for glory, nor riches, nor honour . . . but for freedom alone'.

De Linton, it appears, had a Shakespearean touch with the whitewash brush. But the Declaration is worth more than that. It states that even 'our most tireless Prince, King and Lord Robert' will have their loyalty only while he defends the freedom of the nation. 'Should he give up what he has begun and agree to make our kingdom subject to the King of England or the English, we should exert ourselves at once to drive him out.'

This was at one and the same time a revolutionary and an ancient Celtic principle in 1320. If only it had been maintained in 1707.

TOOM EDWARD

Robert the Bruce died at the age of fifty-five in 1329, apparently of leprosy, and was succeeded by his five-year-old son, David. His extraordinary luck died with him.

Within a few years, Edward III had repudiated the Treaty of Edinburgh. Scotland was invaded by Edward – son of John – Balliol with an English army and the supporters of 'The Disinherited' – barons and knights who had forfeited their Scottish estates in Bruce's reign.

The Scots were defeated at Dupplin Moor, Perthshire, in 1332, and again at Halidon Hill, near Berwick, in 1333, proving again – as Bruce had known well – that they were no match for English archers and cavalry. David fled to France. Balliol was crowned. The Disinherited got their estates back, and other vast territories were handed over to helpful English nobles. In June 1334, the whole of southern Scotland from Haddington in the east to Dumfries in the west was handed over to Edward III as an acknowledgement of his 'great assistance'. Balliol then did homage to his liege lord for his kingdom – or what was left of it.

DAVID II (1329–1371)

Scotland would probably have ceased to exist during this period had it not been that Edward III, like his grandfather, was more interested in conquering France. In 1338, he sailed away to start the Hundred Years' War and claim the French crown.

In 1341, following the recapture of many of the Scots castles from the vassals of Toom Edward by some of David's more enterprising subjects, David himself returned. He bore about as much resemblance to his father as Edward II had borne to his. He was, in other words, a Big Disappointment.

At the bidding of the hard-pressed French, recently massacred at Crécy, David launched an invasion into England, and proved yet again at Neville's Cross in 1346, that an English army could always defeat the Scots in a normal pitched battle. Taken prisoner in the battle, he spent the following eleven years in easy and enjoyable conditions in London, escaping the Black Death then raging in Scotland.

During his captivity, Scotland was governed by a regent – the first of many – Robert the High Steward, son of David's half-sister, Marjorie Bruce. Negotiations over an enormous ransom dragged on till 1354, when the Scots agreed to pay, and the English guaranteed a nine-year truce. At this juncture, however, the French despatched a small force and some 10,000 merks in gold to persuade the Scots barons to break the agreement. 'The Scots,' wrote the chronicler Fordoun, 'will frequently lose a shilling to gain a penny.'

They ravaged the Border and seized Berwick. In return, Edward ravaged the whole countryside between Roxburgh and Edinburgh, regaining Berwick, an action known as Burnt Candlemas from its timing in February, 1356. Scotland had become a mere pawn of the French, and a charred one at that.

A MERCIFUL RELEASE

By the Treaty of Berwick, 1357, King David was released from his captivity and the Scots had to find an increased sum of 100,000 merks in ten yearly instalments. This proved impossible, given the state of the country and the irresponsibility of the King, who spent most of what his subjects raised on riotous and luxurious fun.

The Scots did not approve. There followed a baronial uprising, in which Robert the Steward participated. David, miffed and totally incapable of economy, took himself back to London, where – unbelievably, in view of the twenty years' warfare and devastation his supporters had endured on his behalf – he made an agreement with Edward III whereby, in exchange for a release from all arrears of the ransom, the English King or one of his many sons would succeed David on the Scottish throne if David were childless.

Not surprisingly the Scots parliament refused to ratify this agreement and the crippling taxation to pay off the ransom resumed. Once again however in 1369, the renewal of Edward's French war intervened, causing him to modify the terms in the interests of peace on his northern border.

King David died in 1371, aged forty-six. His long reign had been disastrous by any standard. Warfare and pillage were endemic in the south, economic ruin and incompetent leadership had resulted in breakdown of government, with the nobles taking the law, inevitably, into their own hands. Parliament alone, now called the Three Estates, seemed to advance with the addition of burgh representatives necessitated by the constant need for money.

DARK AND DRUBLIE DAYS

David's miserable reign was the start of that period usually and justifiably called 'Dark and Drublie' by historians, following the great Mackie, who chose the title from a poem by Dunbar. A pattern of mayhem and stagnation was established which was to be repeated *ad nauseam* over the next century.

The chief strands in this grim pattern were: (1) breakdown of central government; (2) increase in baronial power – the local baron was the only possible protection, so a strong baron's following grew; (3) baronial conflicts often involving the Crown; (4) increasing raids by Highland clans into Lowland farming areas; (5) continuing punitive attacks by English armies, invariably involving widespread devastation; (6) continuing Scots raids into England and into the parts of southern Scotland still in English hands under the terms of the agreement of 1334 between Edward Balliol and Edward III; and (7) continuing French involvement.

Who was to blame? Partly Edward III, who lacked both the intelligence and the statesmanship of his grandfather, and who seems to have established the parameters of the pattern by his notorious Burnt Candlemas raid. Partly the feudal system – similar times occurred in other countries. Mainly, perhaps, the all-absorbing greed of the chief men of the Kingdom.

ROBERT II (1371–1390)

David died without issue, and was succeeded by Robert the High Steward (*see* page 57) who, on the other hand, had at least six sons by two wives. Whether for that reason, or because he was already fifty-five and had previously laboured hard to govern the realm as Regent, Robert was an enfeebled and timid monarch, not quite the right style then required for the job.

He was, however, the first of the STEWARTS, so called from his father's hereditary title, High Steward of Scotland, although correctly the family name was FITZ ALAN, descendants of a Breton knight who had come to Scotland in David I's reign. Robert's father, Walter the High Steward, had married Bruce's daughter Marjorie.

To the Scots nobility, the Stewarts, or Fitz Alans, were merely nobles themselves who happened to have made a lucky marriage and come to the Crown by chance, not by reason of ancient lineage, let alone Divine intervention. There was therefore, in their opinion, no particular reason why other nobles should obey them when they proved weak.

Disorder flourished. Chroniclers speak of 'Horrible destructions, burnings and slaughters done through all the Kingdom'. The King's own son, Alexander, aptly nicknamed The Wolf of Badenoch, conducted a private reign of terror in Morayshire. The English burned Dundee and Perth, and ransomed Edinburgh. Two thousand French knights and crossbowmen came across on the invitation, not of King Robert, but of some of his barons. Their intervention was not particularly successful in any way, but their opinion of the Scots is worth a mention: 'Rude and worthless people, like savages, who wish not to be acquainted with anyone, and are too envious of the good fortune of others and suspicious of losing anything themselves.'

ROBERT III (1390–1406)

When the geriatric Robert II had tottered off the throne he was succeeded by the even feebler John, Earl of Carrick, who had already, as Regent for his dad, been superseded as unfit to rule by his own brother Robert, Duke of Albany. Eldest son of Robert II by his first wife, John – who now changed his name to Robert, as if there wasn't enough confusion in the country – had been crippled at a tournament and could no longer ride a horse, a grave disability for a King in a country like Scotland in the fourteenth century. His parents' marriage was open to question, and there were therefore those who believed the legitimate heir to be David, Earl of Strathearn, eldest son of Robert II by his second wife. This did not help.

The new King was a timid, kind old gent who would have been better off in a genteel nursing home in Crieff. Aware of his many shortcomings, he aggravated them by continually deferring to his chief nobles, principally Robert, Duke of Albany (his brother), and Archibald the Grim, Earl of Douglas.

(Scotland's first two dukedoms, created in 1398, were for Albany, the King's brother, and for his eldest son, the Duke of Rothesay.)

Disorder, murder and rapine were again rampant throughout the land. Highlanders slaughtered each other – including a macabre public slaughtering match between Clan Kay and Clan Chattan on Perth links in 1396 – and ravaged into Strathmore. The English won another battle, Homildon Hill in 1402. The degenerate Duke of Rothesay was starved to death in Falkland Castle by Albany and Douglas.

The hopeless King shipped his surviving son James, aged eleven, to France for safety, and the ship was seized by English pirates.

Robert thereupon died: there was little else he could do in the circumstances. His dying wishes, however, are surely among the least pompous ever voiced by anyone who has ever strutted briefly on the stage

of history, even on a stage as liable to imminent collapse and conflagration as the Scottish one, to wit: he was to be buried in a midden, and with the epitaph 'Here lies the worst of the Kings and most wretched of men'.

ROBERT, DUKE OF ALBANY (Regent 1406–1420)

This ambitious, scheming, murderous and incompetent personage with the magnificent title, brother of the previous monarch, now assumed the Royal power as Regent, issuing charters under his own Great Seal, and continuing the disastrous policy of appeasement towards the powerful barons that had characterised the two preceding reigns. This was hardly a surprise, as Albany had often governed on behalf of his brother and father. Virtually nothing was done to secure the release of young James, although Albany's own arrogant and disgusting son, Murdach, was released from England in 1415, and in 1420, on Albany's demise, succeeded to the Regency. It seems obvious that Albany and Son intended a takeover.

Crown lands were alienated like Monopoly money, mainly to the already overmighty nobles, such as the Douglases, who also robbed the Exchequer of its customs revenues from the burghs with impunity. Lawlessness was a way of life: indeed, the only way of life. In 1411, Donald, Lord of the Isles, seized Dingwall, burned Inverness, and was only stopped from plundering Aberdeen by a brave and bloody defence of the town put up by the burghers, local lairds and barons at the Battle of Harlaw. Indeed, it seems to have been the growing anger of such lesser men against the virtual disappearance of Royal authority that was finally instrumental in securing the release of James.

Lollards came to Scotland – the first voice of protest against The Church – and were, not surprisingly, burnt. Barons might be at each others' throats, but nobody with any authority wanted poor priests wandering about questioning the rights of the rich in Church and State: after all, they were making such a good job of things as they were.

JAMES I (1424–1437)

Suddenly, incredibly, the appalling Robertocracy ended, and out of the medieval mist and welter of feudal greed and incompetence stepped a Renaissance Prince, an athlete, a musician, a poet, and as smart as the paint on the first-ever portrait of a King of Scots – and looking unmistakably Scottish as well, despite the seventeen years of English captivity. There is little doubt that James's prolonged English stay had been a matter of collusion between Albany and the English King Henry IV, who used to threaten the wretched Regent with the return of his nephew if he did not maintain the truce between their nations. Henry V's meteoric conquest of France was free from Scots diversions on the French behalf: Agincourt was, in this sense, won on the Scottish Border. James made the most of his opportunities during his enforced stay at the court of Henry, and grew to be one of the most accomplished, civilised men of his age: a real King, such as Scotland had seldom seen before.

When James crossed the Border with his Queen, Lady Joan Beaufort, he was already well aware of the state of his realm and of the urgent need to strengthen Royal authority and put down the over-mighty. His policy, as he expressed it, was: 'If God grant me life, though it be but the life of a dog, there shall be no place in my realm where the key shall not keep the castle and the bracken bush the cow.' The means to this end was to be Parliament, which was first given a thorough reorganisation along contemporary English lines. That many of the unruly nobles were currently absent in France, or now sent into England as hostages for the eventual payment of the King's ransom, was an added advantage.

(It was at this time that Lords – that is, Lords of Parliament – became distinct from the lesser barons, who did not receive individual writs of summons to Parliament.)

ACTION AND REACTION

James and his parliaments were determined to restore justice. Private wars and armies, and the 'Bands of Manrent' – leagues of nobles – that went with them were forbidden. Rebels, and those who did not actively help the King against them, were to be forfeited as well as hanged – that is, their estates would not be allowed to pass to other members of their families. Incompetent sheriffs were replaced. An enquiry was begun into what had happened to all the Royal estates since the reign of David II. A poor man's advocate was instituted. The barons were ordered to get their hands out of the burgh revenues. Weights and measures were regularised. Peace with England continued.

To show he meant business, James had Murdach, Duke of Albany, and his son tried for treason by a tribunal of nobles, and executed. Fifty Highland chiefs, summoned to a parliament at Inverness, were arrested and imprisoned. The Lord of the Isles was, for a time, incarcerated in Tantallon dungeons. The export of considerable revenues to Rome by churchmen was severely restricted, while, as early as 1425, James had instructed abbots and priors to reform their monasteries, 'everywhere defamed and reduced to contempt within our Realm'.

In 1437, despite the bravery of Kate Barlass, James was murdered by a faction of nobles, ostensibly supporters of the rival Strathearn Stewarts (*see* page 61), actually the spearhead of the reaction. By then, James lacked the support even of those lesser men who stood to gain most from strengthened Royal power: they whined and stayed away from parliament because the King taxed them – the Robertocracy had not dared to tax anyone.

It is indicative of the state of Scotland that James was the first King to be murdered there since the Dark Ages.

JAMES II (1437–1460)

The new King, the younger and surviving member of twins, was six years old. Everywhere in Europe, nations were emerging from the Middle Ages: Scotland, with the rapid collapse of everything James I had done to restore law and order, was heading back into the Dark.

A succession of greedy, murderous nobles, with eyes only for their own interests at the expense of the nation's, controlled the young King and schooled him in treachery and murder. Even guests at his own table under safe-conduct were knifed where they sat at meat. Parliament, without a King to back it, was the powerless tool of this or that faction. The Black Douglases and their allies, who now controlled vast estates throughout the realm, were far more powerful than the King when, in 1452, at Stirling, the King knifed William, eighth Earl of Douglas, during dinner. Servants finished him off. The ninth Earl, after burning and looting Stirling in revenge, secured the release from England of the Strathearn Claimant (*see* page 64), but, with the destruction of Strathearn's brothers by James at the Battle of Arkinholme, he was finally exiled and forfeited of all his estates in 1455.

From then on, James, still only twenty-five, ruled his realm with a strong hand. Parliament again passed numerous well-intentioned laws providing for the Royal finance and strong government. Then, with the ill luck that was to dog all the Stewarts, he was killed accidentally by an exploding cannon during the siege of Roxburgh Castle – still in English hands. The siege succeeded, and the castle was destroyed. The spot where James died can be seen today by visitors to Floors Castle, Kelso.

JAMES III (1460–1488)

The Scots as a nation, given to endless squabbling and vying amongst themselves, will put up with anything so long as it doesn't succeed. The Stewarts, now well into their Mark II, or Infantocratic phase, seemed to endure because they developed forms of government that were basically, overwhelmingly, unworkable. Phase I, the Robertocracy, had consisted of government by incompetent geriatrics, who appeased their nobles, taxed nobody, and died in bed. Phase II, Infantocracy, consisted of rule by very young children who spent all their time trying to grow up and attack their overmighty nobles, then, just when they managed to accomplish this, dying a violent death. Repeated from one generation to the next, this recipe for nationwide disorder seems to have guaranteed the Stewarts, if not acceptance – after all, nobody ever is really accepted in Scotland – then sufferance. Between 1406 and 1587 there were nearly 100 years of minority rule and government by Regents.

James, aged nine, was crowned in Kelso Abbey and lived happily for a few years under the tutelage of his mother and Kennedy, Bishop of St Andrews, an apparently virtuous cleric. He was then seized by the Boyds of Kilmarnock, upstarts who proceeded to aggrandise themselves in the normal fashion.

It was they who married James to Margaret, Princess of Denmark in 1469. From this union, by default of dowry, Orkney and Shetland became part of the Kingdom. It was to be many years yet, however, before these Norse, free-living inhabitants experienced the blessings of rule by greedy feudal Scots.

ANOTHER STEWART KING BITES THE DUST

The complex character and policy of James III, and the state of the nation during this turgid period, are matters of some considerable perplexity. That he tried, like Henry Tudor and Louis XI – two contemporary and successful monarchs – to rule through a bevy of clever upstarts, whose company he justifiably preferred to that of his nobles, is borne out by the chroniclers. Unlike Henry and Louis – who were neither Scots nor Stewarts – he failed; and the nobles had the satisfaction of hanging six of his 'favourites' from Lauder Bridge.

(One of them, the architect Cochrane, greatly loathed by the nobles on account of his superior style, died as stylishly as he had lived, dressed in black velvet and with a chain of gold about his neck, protesting with his last breath that he should be hanged with a silken cord, not with 'ane tow of hemp, like ane thief'. Charming fellow.)

James and his companions were, like James I, Renaissance characters, interested in music, poetry and architecture, surrounded by a cast of nobles with considerably less cultural significance than the Picts. They were blamed for everything that was wrong – lawlessness, debased money, plague, famine and high prices – and James suffered accordingly. He was replaced temporarily by his own brother the Duke of Albany in 1482, with English support, and finally by his son James. Following a rash fight against these rebels at Sauchieburn, near Stirling, the King was murdered whilst he lay wounded in Bannockburn Mill.

Yet despite the continuing powerlessness of government, Scotland was slowly prospering at this time. Fine buildings were being built – as at Roslin, Linlithgow and Stirling. Clearly it was possible for some, whether as nobles and their clients, or as burghers, to live well. The basic cause of this paradox was the English.

JAMES IV (1488–1513)

The rebel nobility that won at Sauchieburn had, for once, gone too far. The casual and dastardly murder of the King by some nobleman's lackey passing himself off as a hedge priest was more than even the Scots would condone. Only the Humes and the Hepburns, Earls of Bothwell, made anything out of it: for the rest, there was a backing-down, and the dead James's remaining 'favourites' – principally Elphinstone, Bishop of Aberdeen – were accepted back into the Privy Council of State.

The new King was universally accepted by all ranks – an expression of the feeling that things had gone too far – and, being blessed, unlike his father, with an extrovert, high-spirited, open-handed and fun-loving disposition – such as is rare amongst the Scots – he was quick to endear himself to his subjects, like no King before him. Uniquely for a Mark II Stewart, James, aged fifteen, did not succeed to the throne as an infant – and throughout his reign he sportingly wore an iron chain around his waist as a handicap. There was widespread support as he rode about the land restoring law and order – at least it was a new experience for his subjects. Prosperity increased, particularly in the east coast ports. Edinburgh, now pre-eminently the centre of Royal government, and Aberdeen, were both becoming cities. Dockyards and a navy were built, and numerous noble residences, including Holyrood Palace, were built or extended.

James, always a soft touch, even subsidised an Italian clergyman who claimed to be able to fly to France, and when he crashed on takeoff from Stirling Castle – due, as the aviator explained, to using some hens' feathers in his wings that had inevitably 'drawn him to the midden and not to the skies' – the King made him an abbot for his cheek.

MARRIAGE OF THE THISTLE AND THE ROSE, 1503

Scottish prosperity was the direct consequence of prolonged peace with England. The fifteenth century had not lacked the occasional invasion, and Border feuding went on interminably, but there had been no systematic campaigns of destruction since the time of Edward III. English Kings had been preoccupied with their conquest of, then loss of, France, and then with the Wars of the Roses.

James however, young, bold and intent upon knight-errantry, was keen for military glory, and in 1496 he raided Northumberland on behalf of the English Pretender, Perkin Warbeck. Henry Tudor, that canny man, settled James's hash in 1503 by wedding him with his daughter, Margaret Tudor, and thereby obtaining a 'Treaty of Perpetual Peace'. Asked by his councillors what would happen if a King of Scots eventually fell heir to England as a result of the marriage, Henry replied that in that case Scotland would be a mere appendage of England, as 'the greater would draw the lesser'. The marriage, and the manner in which it was celebrated, was popular in Scotland.

James's energetic style of government is probably best seen in his determined effort to subdue the Highlands and Islands. It took six naval expeditions, a quantity of heavy artillery, and the total extinction and forfeiture of the MacDonald Lords of the Isles before it began to look as if, for the first time, the King's writ would run north and west of the Highland Line.

JAMES THROWS IT ALL AWAY

'The Money' – that is, inflation – had already surfaced as a growing problem in the previous reign, and as James IV spent lavishly on his many projects – and was emulated by his nobles – it became ever more pressing. Scottish taxation was a proven recipe for disaster, as Edward I had discovered to his cost. James raised extra revenue by giving long-term feus, instead of the normal short-term leases, to tenants on Crown estates – thus also benefiting agriculture. He also took many a backhander from the pirates, such as Barton and Wood, who sailed his navy for him and in their spare time preyed upon the mushrooming Dutch and Portuguese merchant fleets. Debasement of 'The Cunzie' – the currency – proceeded apace.

James IV was no smarter than previous Jameses – in fact, he was a bit of a bampot, or wally (which is one reason his nobles liked him better than his predecessors) – but he was the first Lucky King since Robert the Bruce. Bruce, however, had known something James and his nobles rediscovered too late: that the English always defeat the Scots in a pitched battle, unless a clever commander can exploit some chance weakness, as at Bannockburn.

That Superwally, Henry VIII, was now King of England and embroiled in a totally pointless European war. The French called on James for the traditional diversionary attack on the north of England, whereupon the King and his nobles plunged across the Border in pursuit of glory. At Flodden, near Berwick, in 1513, virtually the whole Scots army – including James, thirteen earls and three bishops – was massacred in a three-hour battle against a smaller English force under the Earl of Surrey.

ANOTHER AWFUL REGENCY

Once again, with tiresome predictability, all the progress of one reign was followed by a minority, and a welter of feuds, this time between the Red Douglases, led by the Earl of Angus, and the Hamiltons, captained by the Earl of Arran. Angus promptly married the widowed Margaret Tudor and secured the infant King.

Into this unsavoury Scotch broth stepped a very grand Frenchman, John, Duke of Albany, son of the Albany who had temporarily replaced James III with English help. Albany was heir presumptive to the throne, and was appointed Regent in 1515. He was in every way a French grandee, spoke only French, and pursued a French policy of further embroiling the Scots in English invasions whilst his French masters and Henry VIII gavotted about in a tangled web in Europe. He took frequent long vacations in France, emptied the impoverished treasury maintaining a vast French retinue that included a private company of actors and a body of Italian trumpeters. Eventually, in 1524, with the Borders ravaged and both Kelso and Jedburgh Abbeys burned on Henry's orders, Albany departed for France in the sulks, miffed by the reluctance of the remaining Scots nobles to invade England.

Throughout his Regency, the customary mayhem and murder proceeded unchecked, memorably when, in 1520, the Douglases and Hamiltons held a pitched battle in Edinburgh High Street.

Angus and his henchmen, having the boy King in gilded captivity after 1524, ran the country very much as they pleased till 1528, when James escaped from their clutches.

JAMES V (1513–1542)

Scots were ignominiously defeated at Solway Moss in 1542, many of the nobles refusing to fight and others surrendering quickly. James died a few weeks later.

James, sixteen when he took power from Angus, and nearly thirty-one when he died, was a complex combination of Stewart flair and Tudor ruthlessness. The ruthlessness was directed, justifiably, against his nobles. Angus, driven from his mighty fortress at Tantallon, near North Berwick, took refuge in England. Border barons like the Maxwells, Scotts and Armstrongs, who obeyed no king and who could well bring about massive English retaliation by their cross-Border raids, were summarily hanged. The Royal fleet visited Orkney, Lewis, Skye and many other remote and inaccessible parts, taking local chiefs captive to Edinburgh. The King was said to have had a list of over 300 nobles who could be hanged for treason or heresy whenever he wished. To such, James was a hated tyrant.

To his lesser subjects, however, James was 'The Gudeman of Ballengeich', who, with youthful high spirits and appropriate failings, travelled incognito around his realm learning much about its people. He was the King who set up the Court of Session, in Edinburgh, the first central civil court, with a judiciary paid for by taxing the Church – a Church that was not only neglectful of its work among ordinary folk, but corrupt, and richer by far than the Crown itself, possessing about half the total wealth of the country.

Inflation and continuous overspending by the Crown and the nobility made it inevitable that, at a time when Henry VIII and other princes were confiscating church lands and wealth, the Protestant cause would find support in Scotland. A Protestant, Patrick Hamilton, was burned in 1528 at St Andrews. Despite Henry VIII's continual promptings to follow his lead, James maintained the old religion and – by his two marriages – the French alliance. But there was growing noble support for a Protestant, and thereby pro-English, party.

When the ageing Henry suspected that James was advancing towards active participation in a Catholic Alliance against him, he invaded. The

THE REFORMATION

James's demise, true to the well-tried Stewart formula – whereby a young and vigorous monarch was just getting his act together when he dies and leaves an infant in charge – was more than usually disastrous. It introduced two new ingredients: (1) his successor was a girl, the one-week-old Mary; and (2) the Reformation.

The Scots, as we have seen, had been bickering and murdering each other since the Dark Ages for good, old-fashioned, worldly reasons: they needed religious quarrels like the Ethiopians need famine. However, although the destruction of the Catholic Church and its immense wealth was very much a matter of traditional greed, and a heaven-sent answer to the pressing financial problems of the nobles and Crown, the Reformation was not wholly without religious significance.

The Church itself, at its Provincial Council of 1549, admitted appalling corruption, secularism and virtual breakdown of its ministry. This is hardly surprising, as it had been run as Big Business since Canmore times. The Reformers, at least some of them, were inspired by the Scriptures – now circulating in the vernacular and available for the first time ever. But the fact remains that their motives were very mixed, many of them were paid by the English, and the real force behind the movement came from the same greedy class that had activated every rebellion since the time of Alexander III. Some of these 'Lords of the Congregation' claimed to be truly reformed characters, but their religion, like their patriotism, proceeded from the purse rather than the heart.

THE ROUGH WOOING

Hamilton, Earl of Arran, heir presumptive to the Crown through descent from a daughter of James II, was next in the long line of greedy and incompetent Regents. He posed as a Protestant, chiefly to spite his enemy, the evil Beaton, Cardinal Archbishop of St Andrews. The pro-English stance was strengthened by the return of the Solway Moss fugitives (*see* page 72) and the Earl of Angus, all of them bribed with English gold.

That ageing megalomaniac, Henry VIII, had conceived the notion of acquiring Scotland à la Edward I, by betrothing the infant Scots Queen Mary to his son, and this was agreed by the Treaty of Greenwich, 1543. However, as in times past, the French were altogether too powerful to let this pass. Arran and his chums were – correctly – accused of selling the country to the English. Cardinal Beaton threatened to annul Arran's father's marriage and thereby make him a bastard – which, arguably, though in a looser sense, he was already.

Thereupon, the Regent caved in. Beaton and Mary of Guise – widow of the late King James – joined the Regency Council, and the pro-French Catholic party were in the ascendant.

Thwarted, Henry unleashed 'The Rough Wooing' in 1544. A fleet and two armies under the Earl of Hertford devastated, looted and destroyed Edinburgh, four Border abbeys and everything else that attracted them. This, far from persuading the Scots that the English were nice people, drove them further into the embrace of France. Protestantism became synonymous with treason. Beaton proceeded to burn Reformers, the foremost amongst them being George Wishart in 1546.

But the Reformers were by now too strong to be cowed. Two months later, a group of Protestant Fife lairds hanged the Cardinal and seized his castle at St Andrews. They held it for a year against all comers until a French fleet took it by bombardment. John Knox, one of the religious leaders, and other captives, were despatched to the French galleys.

LITTLE FRANCE

Scotland in the mid sixteenth century bears more than a passing resemblance to one of those troublesome, savage parts of the nineteenth-century Dark Continent that the rival British and French Empires strove to colonise, flooding it with their bright gewgaws and inappropriate fashions. From 1548 till 1560, it was France's turn.

In France, the House of Guise was in power. In England, following the death of Henry VIII, Hertford, now Duke of Somerset, assumed control. He renewed his Rough Wooing, defeating the Scots again at the Battle of Pinkie in 1548, but was totally outmanoeuvred diplomatically when, by the Treaty of Haddington, the French removed the little girl Queen Mary to France, betrothed her to the Dauphin and sent thousands of battle-hardened French troops to rebuff the English suitor.

Thereafter, the French virtually took over the government. Arran, now made Duke of Châtelherault, was brow-beaten and bribed into giving away the Regency to the Queen Mother, Mary of Guise, although he was allowed to keep all the Crown property, including the Crown jewels that he had filched during his period in office. French troops were garrisoned in the Royal castles and Frenchmen held the great offices of state. The wedding of Mary and the Dauphin Francis in 1558, was followed by a reversal of Mary of Guise's previous toleration of Protestants.

Shortly afterwards, however, the Protestant Elizabeth succeeded the Catholic Mary Tudor on the English throne. The French, finally over-reaching themselves, claimed the English throne for Mary and Francis, as, in Catholic eyes, Elizabeth, daughter of Anne Boleyn was illegitimate. The Reformers, now once more assured of English help, rioted and vandalised churches in Perth, and the Lords of the Congregation rose in rebellion.

In January 1560, an English fleet dropped anchor in the Forth, preventing reinforcements from reaching the Guise government. In April,

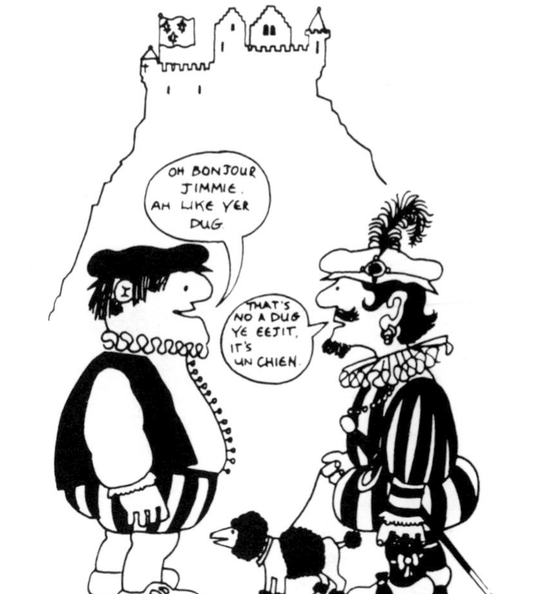

an English army crossed the Border. The Regent Mary died in June, and England and France signed the Treaty of Edinburgh in July. Under its terms, Elizabeth was acknowledged Queen of England, and both English and French troops withdrew from Scotland.

Unlikely as it would have seemed at the time, this was in fact the last time an English army – as distinct from a United Kingdom one – invaded Scotland. It was also the last of the 'Auld Alliance' between Scotland and France.

MARY, QUEEN OF SCOTS (1560–1567)

The practical (as distinct from religious or spiritual) significance of the Reformation was that it extended the politically active section of the population. The 'Reformation Parliament' that met in August 1560, was full of minor barons and lairds, a group that James I had tried in vain to involve in the political process. The Reformers were strong in Fife, Lothian and the east coast burghs. Both Knox and Wishart were, at one time, teachers. The Parliament abolished Popery and set up Protestantism, though the legality of its Acts and membership are open to question, and neither these nor the Treaty of Edinburgh were ever confirmed by Mary.

The Queen, last of the Mark II Stewarts, was archetypally charming, headstrong and tragically unlucky. She arrived in Scotland in 1561, a nineteen-year-old girl, suddenly widowed, virtually friendless, leaving behind forever a happy girlhood spent in carefree French châteaux, to face the same old greedy feuds that her predecessors had grappled with, but worsened now by the additional ingredient of religious intolerance. To the customary overmighty nobles – Châtelherault, now again a Protestant, and Lord James Stewart, a bastard of James V's (later Earl of Moray) – who fancied they might well take the Crown, were added the demagogue preachers and crowds of Protestant zealots, backed by the Lords of the Congregation.

Mary was wholly unprepared for all this. Only a wise marriage could have saved her, yet even in such matters the young Queen was an innocent.

And ever in the background, cousin Elizabeth plotted and contrived to encompass the downfall of the woman who could, given a strong Catholic uprising, supplant her on the English throne.

Mary's two Scottish marriages – first to Henry, Lord Darnley, a Lennox Stewart and total weed (1565), second to his supposed murderer the Earl of Bothwell, a rascally adventurer – were both personally and politically

disastrous. In July 1567, she was imprisoned by the 'Confederate Lords' in Lochleven Castle, and forced to demit the Crown to her infant son James. The following year she escaped to England, there to drag out a life of perilous imprisonment until Elizabeth had her executed in 1587.

Few more evil tales of greed and bigotry can be found in history, even in Scottish history.

JAMES VI (1567–1625)

Antonia Fraser, in her book on James, aptly described the nobility as 'wolves circling around a lone traveller' – (that is, the Monarch) – 'ever menacing, ever ready to pounce at a hint of weakness'.

The Reformation merely added hyenas to this pack. The howling was louder, but the amount of Christian charity demonstrated was nil. As elsewhere, the Reformation merely increased bloodshed, bigotry and nastiness, and the national disgrace that was Mary's reign is a clear indication of this.

Bothwell's real fault had been that he had had no support among the wolves and hyenas: the pack pounced, replacing Mary – whom Elizabeth and others believed they had cause to fear – with the infant James. It was, in other words, business as usual for the Scots nobility and their lackeys.

James, one of the most singular Princes ever to reign, grew up a rickety, wise wee boy, stuffed with learning by ferocious Presbyterian turors. He was completely deprived of friends or affection, until in 1579, he developed an understandable passion for the first person ever to befriend him, a French cousin, Esmé Stewart. Until 1583, when he took personal control, his life was that of a bone, seized and fought over endlessly by rival wolf packs and so-called Regents. The Hamiltons, Douglases, Morays, Mars, Lennoxes, and various unsavoury combinations of nobles and ranting Presbyterian divines, all fought and squabbled in the name of one thing or another and were all – with the possible exception of Andrew Melville, the Presbyterian – activated by self-aggrandisement. Royal courts were powerless against such groups and grandees with their private armies and jurisdictions, and the remoter regions were totally beyond the pale. Since Flodden (1513), there had only been fourteen years of strong government – during the personal rule of James V – and, as a result, the powers of the nobility had reached new heights.

Yet, through all the years of raids and the humiliations he suffered, the whimsical, pedantic James sharpened his wits and kept to his own course: the establishment of an absolute monarchy and the English succession.

power and patronage, on a wider and unprecedented level, the loyalty of the Scots nobility was truly something wonderful to behold.

It was just at this point in their successful development that previous Jameses would have got themselves assassinated or killed in battle, leaving some tiny bairn in charge. 'But Jamie the Saxt was a wiser chield than them aa', for all his curious quirks. And what was even rarer, he was lucky.

KINGCRAFT

Despite his eccentricities – the wonder was he wasn't totally mad – and his quirky obsessions with thorny theological abstractions, witches and demons (the case of the North Berwick witches, 1591, fascinated him), despite the extreme impoverishment of the Crown following decades of peculation and robbery by nobles and regents, James arranged a kingly marriage for himself to Anne of Denmark. To lay on fitting celebrations for this celebration in 1590, the King had to send begging letters to the nobility and baronage for everything from meat to plate and carriages, and even had to borrow a decent pair of tights from the Earl of Moray. Despite the continuing sporadic lawlessness of the Wizard Earl of Bothwell, and the Gowrie Conspiracy of 1600, by the end of his Scottish reign James was, like most of the previous Jameses, getting his act together.

Contributing to this were: (1) the King's own 'Kingcraft', as he termed it, a mixture of astuteness, bribes, threats, flattery, chicanery and commonsense that was all his own; (2) sound advisers, such as Sir John Maitland of Thirlestane; (3) a victory of sorts over the extreme Presbyterians, who claimed – like medieval Popes – to have supreme power over the King himself; (4) a happy and fruitful marriage; (5) the continuing rise in political importance of the lesser barons and prosperous burghers; and (6) the Act of Annexation, 1587, which, though it weakened the Episcopate that James wished to maintain as a bulwark against the Presbyterians, annexing to the Crown all the extant Church lands and revenues, gave the King a power and patronage that all his predecessors had lacked.

The nobility was not slow to realise that, when a King had lands and wealth to bestow, it was now in their interests to practise the unaccustomed arts of the courtier and royalist. A new ball game was beginning, and after 1603, with the sudden further increase in Royal

JAMES VI AND I, KING OF GREAT BRITAIN

If, in 1567 at the beginning of his reign as an infant in Scotland, a thousand gambling men had been asked to stake their money on James living to become the absolute ruler of Scotland *and* England, few would have ventured a bawbee. Yet not only did he do this, but he also, uniquely, died of old age.

Understandably, James wasted no time getting out of Scotland when the news finally reached him that Elizabeth had died and left him her Kingdom. Nor did he return again, except once, briefly, in 1617. For him, it was, as he said himself: 'like a poor man wandering about forty years in a wilderness and barren soil, and now arrived at the land of promise'. Anyone who has followed this book thus far will well understand his feelings. On his leisurely journey south through England, he lodged at magnificent mansions built for peace and splendour, two commodities in perennial short supply in his homeland, where even the greatest castle was still a gaunt, bare fortress.

In a sense, Scotland ceased to be a nation in 1603, because it was thereafter governed from London. As the King himself put it: 'Here I sit and govern with my pen . . . which others could not do by the sword.' However, the English strenuously resisted his attempts at a more complete union, and Scotland therefore retained its own laws and Parliament, although that body, unlike its English counterpart, was largely a rubber stamp of whoever was in power, controlled hand and foot through a committee, the Lords of the Articles, that arranged all its business. James ruled Scotland through this, and through his Scottish Privy Council, composed of Royal nominees.

From 1597 till 1637, Scotland lived at peace – a state which in places like the Borders had been unknown since 1286. Only religious bickering remained alive from all the old feuds, and in this James exercised his astute understanding of his countrymen's character. He persuaded recalcitrant clerics to accept his Episcopalian 'Five Articles' by awarding increases of stipend to those who fell into line.

The Scots loved and revered him, as they love and revere only those who make good abroad. It was a time of new opportunities for those with energy to seize them. New men bought Nova Scotia baronetcies. Fifty thousand Lowlanders settled on Ulster plantations, and as many more went a-soldiering in the religious wars that were racking contemporary Europe – and which James was determinted to prevent at home.

With all his faults, James, that most unlikely King, was the greatest and wisest Prince ever to rule Scotland, and as a Christian Prince with more claim to that title than many that have vaunted it, it is not unfitting that the great Authorised Version of the Bible that bears his name is a lasting memorial.

The English had been trying to stop Scots raids into their country since the Dark Ages, and now they were paying them to come. It was a mad world: a world of religious mania that had afflicted Europe for long, and which both Elizabeth and James, in their different ways, had striven hard to keep at bay. Charles, that serious, prim and rather dim King, was incapable of coping with it, and so were his advisers.

CHARLES I (1625–1649)

Charles was a mistake. He had to replace Henry, Prince of Wales, his popular and energetic elder brother who unfortunately died in 1612. Charles had all the advantages his father never had as a lad, except one: he lacked a sense of humour. Though he was born in Dunfermline, the Scots regarded him as a foreigner, and were therefore in no mood to be pushed around when he started interfering in their religion with his Prayer Book of 1637.

James had (just) managed to cajole the Scots into accepting Bishops. He well knew from experience that Presbyterianism was a political threat to Royal power. But Charles was too thick to grasp that his northern subjects could not, in those days, be forced to do anything: they had to be wheedled, conned and bribed, as James had done.

Prayer Book riots led to the National Covenant in 1638. Multitudes of all ranks flocked to sign it – some with their blood. The Scots, having been kept at peace for an abnormal period of forty years, were bent on rebellion. Soldiers of fortune who had been butchering Catholics in Europe for many years returned home fast. The Glasgow Assembly met and abolished Episcopacy, illegally. The outbreak of Rampant Presbyterianism – a particularly virulent form of the Scottish endemic disease, Endless Bickering – was uncontrollable, particularly as Charles was embroiled at the same time with the English Puritans.

In 1639 and 1640, the Covenanters invaded England – 'The Bishops Wars' – and because Charles had for eleven years been pig-headedly trying to govern England without its Parliament, he was unable to raise a proper army to oppose them. The Covenanters had a ball. The Estates – the Scots Parliament, hitherto a Royal rubber stamp – took power in Scotland. Charles was forced to recall his English Parliament in a vain attempt to raise money, but they voted £300,000 instead to the Presbyterians for their pains.

SOURFACED ARCHIBALD

The Presbyterian bigots who, through their General Assembly, ruled the Lowlands during this period of rebellion, exercised a power approaching that of a modern police state. They were The Saved, predestined by God to be right, both in belief and in conduct, and the opposition were therefore The Damned. Common rules of ethics didn't apply – indeed, it was sacrilege even to show mercy to the enemy. The Damned were not just theological enemies, they were traitors, and it was one's religious duty to exterminate all such. Witch burnings became weekly events.

Behind all these raving fanatics lurked the inevitable nobles, principally the Earl of Argyll, that archetypal dour, calculating, grasping Presbyterian, aptly termed in Gaelic 'Sourfaced Archibald'. Moderates among the lesser men were trapped in the reign of terror of the Saints, as they called themselves.

Only the Marquis of Montrose for a time succeeded in combating the tyranny, in so doing remaining true to his original signing of the Covenant, which had, in fact, enjoined loyalty to Charles – their original banners had proclaimed 'For Crown and Covenant'. When this was replaced by the fanatics' 'Jesus and No Quarter', Montrose, failing to get support anywhere else, raised a Highland army and brought over Scots from Antrim.

For a while, Charles's fortunes in his English civil war improved. The hard-pressed English Puritan Parliament concluded with the Scots rebels the Solemn League and Covenant (1643), whereby, in return for Scots military aid, they undertook to establish Presbyterianism in England. Charles was then defeated, fled – Heaven alone knows why – to Scotland, refused point blank to institute Presbyterianism in England, was handed over to the English (1647), and was eventually executed by them in 1649.

Montrose, meanwhile, had been defeated with great slaughter at Philiphaugh, near Selkirk. But, though Sourfaced Archibald and the

bigots were now completely in power in Edinburgh, the fanatics had shot their bolt. Their co-religionists in London had been superseded by Cromwell and his New Model Army. And Cromwell, towering high above all the crazy sectaries, had no time for bigots.

Cromwellian General Monk put down a Royalist rising with fire and sword: forts were built, military police were in control; there were passports, weapon licences, forfeitures and fines.

It was sound, sensible government, and better than the sectaries deserved. But an essential part of the old Scotland had gone for ever. The unique personal contact between Crown and subject that had characterised the best periods of the Scots monarchy, at its apogee in the reign of James VI, was never to be again. No sovereign King ever again came to Scotland: and who, in the circumstances, could blame them?

The Godly, like later totalitarian regimes, now resorted to a series of drastic purges, excluding from their elect ranks – and in particular from their army – all who had incurred Divine displeasure. The effect of this was to send away many sound, professional troops, and replace them with ranting windbags, many of them sons of the manse. It was hardly the best preparation for an encounter with Oliver Cromwell.

They also clutched at straws. Having contributed largely to the execution of Charles I, a group now formed to proclaim his son King. When this precocious youth arrived in Scotland, they subjected him to endless tirades on religious matters, and made him promise to impose Presbyterianism on all his realms. The young Charles had nothing to lose, and was even then probably developing a proper – and hardly surprising – cynicism in such matters. His only real supporter, Montrose, had been executed in 1650, after raising another hopeless rising in the far north. The bigots now split, amidst a welter of mutual recrimination and spite, between those who thought young Charles would be a Covenanted King, once restored, and the more extreme group, called Protesters or Whiggamores, who were totally anti-monarchist.

So Charles and his Godly army invaded England, and were savagely defeated at the Battle of Worcester in 1651. What happened thereafter was very much the shape of things to come as far as Scotland was concerned. Cromwell incorporated Scotland with England, confiscated Crown property and abolished some of the feudal jurisdictions – directed at reducing the power of the Highland chiefs, where the only real opposition remained. The General Assembly was closed down by one Colonel Cotterel – not before time, in the circumstances – and it did not meet again until 1690. In lieu of a Scots Parliament, thirty MPs were sent to Westminster, and free trade for Scots ships and merchants was instituted – much to the dislike of the English. In the Highlands, the

CHARLES II (1660–1685)

The restoration of the Monarchy in 1660 was greeted, as in England, with universal rejoicing. A King would bridle the bigots and their kangaroo courts, the Kirk Sessions, and there would be no more English garrisons. Argyll was beheaded for treason. The nobles had had more than enough of their alliance with the Presbyterians. North of the Tay, where the Presbyterians had never had any popular following, the people welcomed the return of Episcopacy. Many of the bigots themselves believed that Charles, a Covenanted King (*see* page 82), would favour their cause. The Presbyterian champion, Revd James Sharpe, minister of Crail, went to London to put their case, and returned as Archbishop of St Andrews. Parliament, restored, was subservient and thoroughly counter-revolutionary.

But it was, and was ever to continue, government from London, exercised through the Lords of the Articles (*see* page 79) and a King's Commissioner, the Earl (later Duke) of Lauderdale, a renegade Presbyterian, who, like Charles, knew enough of James VI's 'Kingcraft' to temper government with a sound knowledge of the governed. There was only one fly in this Balm of Gilead: the Covenanters.

These were now reduced to a strange and, it must be said – despite the continuing intolerant, mad bigotry of their ministers – heroic people located almost entirely in the remote, anciently British, areas of southern Strathclyde and Galloway. They were almost all simple, uneducated folk, shepherds, used to lonely communion with their hill lands and the Books of the Prophets and the Psalms. They were, apart from some of their ministers, not the ranting burghers and Kirk Session tyrants of the preceding period, yet their demands were the same as ever, and as laid down in the Solemn League and Covenant of 1643, when Presbyterian power had been at its height: a Covenanted King to impose Presbyterianism on all three Kingdoms, and, failing that, No King but King Jesus.

COVENANTERS

Claverhouse's Dragoons and the Covenanters. That time is commemorated by many a memorial in the churchyards and lonely hillsides of the south-west – the grave of the Wigtown Martyrs, tied to a stake in the Solway by Grierson of Lagg being one such – but it was a time too, as in many such bitter ideological conflicts, when truth itself was, and is, the first casualty.

Lauderdale's religious settlement owed much to James VI. Episcopacy there must be, but otherwise Kirk Sessions and Presbyteries remained; there was to be no Prayer Book and no interference in doctrine. Letters of Indulgence were issued which allowed ministers to remain in their charges even if they would not make the required submissions of acceptance, provided only that they were peaceable. In all this, Lauderdale was at pains to temper the counter-revolutionary sympathies of the Royalists.

But he could only go so far. When a remnant of extreme Presbyterian ministers refused to have any truck with the new church establishment, they were ejected. These were then the leaders who brought the country folk of the south-west to worship in the hills in Conventicles. As similar groups of religious extremists had compassed the overthrow of Charles I, it is hardly surprising that the government now chose to treat the Covenanters as a political threat to the Royalist establishment, and their preaching as incendiary sedition – which some of it certainly was.

Dragoons and Highland troops were sent into the south-west. There were small risings, put down so simply that the government might have seen the Covenanters were no major threat. The zealots murdered Archbishop Sharpe, and, briefly, seized Glasgow. So the situation worsened, and such Covenanters as were left after the shootings, fighting, and transportings to the West Indies as slaves, became more and more extreme. These, often called Cameronians after one of their leaders, Richard Cameron, established contact with the Dutch – Calvinists themselves and currently anti-English – hoping for their aid to impose the Covenants.

Meanwhile, the Catholic James, Duke of York, Charles's silly brother, had replaced Lauderdale as King's Commissioner for Scotland. The so-called 'Killing Times' began: open warfare in the south-west between

JAMES VII and II (1685–1688)

James, at the age of fifty-two, was, like his father Charles I, incapable of understanding that personal bravery and religious devotion are no substitutes for 'Kingcraft'. His brother, Charles II, had known better, and had got away with being a Catholic by the simple expedient of keeping it secret. James was not only an open Catholic, but from the start of his reign was plainly intent on restoring his Kingdoms to that faith as soon as possible, a policy so politically unrealistic that it is small wonder his reign was short.

The Renwickites – James Renwick, a youth from Moniaive in Dumfriesshire, a graduate of Edinburgh and Groningen, took over leadership of the 'Faithful Remnant' after the execution of Cameron and Cargill – were in open rebellion, and held kangaroo courts, trying and executing such of their opponents as fell into their hands. Argyll landed from Holland, tried to raise a rebellion, bickered, was unpopular, and was executed. Covenanters, packed into the dungeons of Dunottar Castle, near Stonehaven, were subjected to torture. Yet the country as a whole was prepared to thole James rather than face another civil war, and his Declaration of Indulgence, permitting religious freedom to all persuasions – though clearly seen as merely a step to Catholic supremacy – was accepted even by Presbyterians.

Events in England forced James to desert his Kingdoms in December, 1688. Renwick, executed on the Maiden in Edinburgh in February, was the last person in Scotland to be killed for religion (or was it treason?). Claverhouse, now Viscount Dundee, raised a Highland army to fight for James, defeated the government redcoats at the Battle of Killiecrankie, but was killed in the battle. The Covenanters, now formed into a pro-government regiment called the Cameronians, had their revenge by soundly defeating the dead Claverhouse's Highlanders – who outnumbered them four to one – at Dunkeld.

The Convention of Estates, 1689, offered the Scots Crown to William and Mary – who already had the English one – on one condition: Episcopacy was to be abolished. The Calvinist Dutchman promptly accepted. It was the end of the road for religious warriors in Scotland.

The Scottish nobility had at last found a way of engaging its energetic greed that didn't involve the death and destruction of the rest of the nation.

THE ECONOMIC AND CULTURAL MIX

The Covenanters had been a small minority in a remote and inaccessible part of the Kingdom, yet, despite their faults, it was they who maintained the spirit of independence at a time when Scotland had become a mere poverty-stricken appendage of England, and a humbled one at that. Famine and beggary were rife. Agriculture was still in the Dark Ages of bare subsistence, though surpluses existed in some places and were traded from one part of the country to another. Highlanders, for example, drove their surplus cattle regularly to markets in Perthshire and Stirlingshire, and returned home with needed meal, malt and cloth. In the burghs, medieval restrictive practices stultified trade and commercial development. Overseas trade was still typically a Third World process, exporting raw materials cheap – hides, salt fish, wool, fleeces, coal, oats, etc. – and importing costly finished goods and luxuries.

Yet, despite the wars and religion, and chiefly as the nobles turned from political and religious aggression to commercial and industrial development, changes came quickly in the latter part of the seventeenth century. Cromwell's Union had shown the way. Glasgow started to flourish, and – even after the withdrawal of trading equality with England, when Cromwell's Union was terminated in 1660 – continued to trade illicitly in tobacco, sugar, mahogany and oranges with the English colonies in America and the West Indies. Acts of Parliament fostered a host of new private ventures, from woollen and linen mills to paper making, coal mining and iron founding. Joint stock companies became the fashion as religion went out, the Bank of Scotland, founded in 1695, being the most famous. Burghs of Barony and country fairs mushroomed, allowing landowners successfully to challenge the medieval burgh monopolies. Schools were, in the more prosperous parts of the country, established for all boys. The only creative art at which the Scots – and more anciently, the Picts – had ever excelled was architecture and building. It reached its apogee in the final and remarkable flowering of the tower house.

THE DARIEN SCHEME

Whilst the nobles turned to the economic development of their estates, to joint stock companies, and to speculation, as new outlets for their energies, the energetic ordinary poor Scotsman turned increasingly to emigration. An abortive scheme in James VI's reign to colonise Nova Scotia had resulted only in baronets, but, from Cromwell's time onwards, prisoners of war, Covenanters, paupers, vagrants and law-breakers were transported forcibly to the New World. It soon became clear to these enterprising persons – and to their friends and relations when they got their letters – that the opportunities available there to 'criminals' were far better than those for honest, law-abiding folk at home. Increasing numbers followed them voluntarily, many going as 'indentured labourers' – like nineteenth-century coolies – bound to a master for a number of years, then free to make their own livelihood in New England or the West Indies.

Both these trends helped fire and finance the disastrous Darien Scheme of 1695–1700. It attempted to plant a Scots colony and entrepôt in Panama. It failed, ruining thousands of backers both great and small. As usual, the blame was laid on the English, though the Scots merchandise – including such products as wigs and heavy worsted stockings – would hardly have gone down a bomb with the Panamanians.

That the scheme ever got off the ground at all is, however, the main point: the Scots, having for the most part held nothing more in their sights throughout their history than the murder and robbery of their neighbours, were now raising their sights at other targets. And those who saw clearest and furthest in this direction saw that as long as Scotland and England remained politically separate, with the English Parliament in supreme control of overseas trade and expansion, the Scots were not going to get far.

The choice after Darien was clear to all such perspicacious people: if you can't beat them, join them. It was the same choice that Malcolm Canmore had had to make in 1074 at Abernethy (*see* page 25).

WILLIAM AND MARY (1688–1702)

William was no more a Scottish King and no more interested in Scotland than any other Dutchman, but he happened to be married to the eldest daughter of James VII. He was not even particularly interested in England, but furiously engaged in prolonged and complicated European wars against the French. His main function in Scotland was to be blamed for things that went wrong, such as the Darien Scheme and the Massacre of Glencoe in 1692, when the MacDonalds were singled out as an example of what would happen to any other Highland clans suspected of being Jacobites, or supporters of the deposed James. In fact, contrary to popular belief, many of them escaped. Perhaps the resulting outcry was another sign that times were changing, and the old ways, which undoubtedly included massacres of, or by, Highlanders, were on the way out.

The most unexpected aspect of William's reign in Scotland is the emergence of the Scottish Parliament as a free, vigorous and surprisingly responsible assembly, following the abolition of the Lords of the Articles – that monarchically appointed committee which had always controlled and largely transacted all parliamentary business.

Following the immense economic losses incurred in the Darien Scheme, the Estates – that is, Parliament – determined on a patriotic gambit, and, whilst the English Parliament settled the Succession to their own satisfaction on Anne, Mary's sister, and failing issue from her, on the Hanoverian Electress Sophia, the Scots declined to do any such thing. Whether the ensuing obduracy and stushie were real, or elaborate play-acting to wring from the English what the dominant class in Scotland most wanted, is a matter for speculation.

For the dominant English squirearchy, however, Scotland only had a nuisance value now. It was a nuisance that had to be Scotched.

'THE END OF AN AULD SANG', 1707

The failure of the Darien Scheme sealed the fate of the Scottish Parliament, and with it the fate of Scotland as a separate nation – although by the end of the seventeenth century that nation was hardly any longer a separate viable entity. What the politically and economically active class desired now above all was complete commercial equality with England. The English saw no reason at all to share their prosperity with a poverty-stricken appendage of greedy, oat-eating Presbyterian beggars. Their involvement in the War of the Spanish Succession, however, gave the Scots nobility, through the newly liberated Estates, the chance to play an old game for the last time. Scotland would choose its own monarch, probably James VIII – son of James VII – and the French would again have a base to attack England from the north.

The various acts and ploys in this play-acting ended with the Act of Union, 1707. Scotland closed its own Parliament for ever in return for the coveted commercial equality. They were allowed to have forty-five MPs at Westminster – one more than Cornwall. The Presbyterians were bought off by English agreement to a Scots Presbyterian Established Church – which was less than fair to the whole country north of the Tay, where Presbyterians were in a small minority. The baronial jurisdictions and the privileges of the Royal Burghs were upheld. The great nobles, who should have been the country's leaders – Hamilton, Argyll and Queensberry – received English peerages, pensions, and loud cheers in London. Venal Scots MPs received their fill of pensions and handouts from the £398,085 and 10 shillings that was trundled northwards in carts to square the accounts. A service of Thanksgiving was held in St Paul's Cathedral.

It was the biggest sell-out in history, and definitely worth celebrating in England. A few cartloads of money had achieved what Edward I and Henry VIII, amongst many others, had failed to do. The Scots had ceased to be a nation, and, in the eyes of Europe, had ceased to be worthy of respect.

But the Highlanders at least went down fighting. 1746 was not 1707. Which is why the Highlander, despite over a hundred years of tartan trivialisation, is still worthy of respect.

EPILOGUE, 1745–1746

There remained, as ever, the Highlands. From the time of Malcolm Canmore and the establishment of the feudal Kingdom, the Highlanders and the Islesmen had remained outside, ruled by their own chiefs, living within a different social, linguistic and cultural structure, protected by topography and their own ferocious skills in battle. From James IV's time onwards, with the strength of fleets and firearms, the Kings of Scots had been able to restrict their former total freedom from government interference. But still they remained apart, and in the seventeenth and early eighteenth centuries they were both culturally and economically healthier than their beggarly fellow-countrymen in the Lowlands. Montrose and Claverhouse had recruited troops there, wild, impetuous fighters in the ancient mode who scared redcoats witless – as at Killiecrankie – but who were in no sense disciplined soldiers and were prone to disappear fast into their distant glens and mountains with booty.

Here, paradoxically, were the last hopes of the Stewarts, when Prince Charles Edward in 1745 attempted to turn back the clock on the Jacobite behalf. The Highlanders had resisted the Stewart Kings and all other English or French-speaking Kings of Scots since time immemorial, but for religion's sake – and for the booty and the fun, of course – many turned out for the Prince.

And signed the death warrant of their own unique society. The Battle of Culloden, April 1746, was not just the last Highland battle; it was the last of the Highlands, in the same sense as 1707 was the last of Scotland the nation. Their language, dress, weapons and social structure were thereafter proscribed, and within two generations they were being driven from their ancient territories to make way for sheep, betrayed even by their hereditary chiefs – by then transformed into English milords. Then after the sheep, it was the deer and the grouse. And now its the tourists and the white settlers.

CONCLUSION

Secured by Chubb doors and multiple electronic devices in Edinburgh Castle, lie the Scottish Crown Jewels. Over a million people a year file through that small room. What they see there is virtually all that remains of a once proud nation – excepting The Church and The Law, which are maintained in ossified form by entrenched, powerful interests. It is fitting that these ancient symbols of royal power remain, because Scotland was better served by her Kings than by her nobles, clerics or people.

Like other nations that have gone out of existence, the Scots blame their misfortunes on others, the English being the universal scapegoat. Yet this is manifestly absurd. England's policy from the earliest times was to safeguard its northern border, not to conquer what it didn't want. You might as well blame the Romans. The Scottish nobility are often blamed too, with considerable justification. But in reality, they only demonstrated on a grand scale what are in fact national characteristics: a disastrous predeliction for endless bickering and internecine strife, and a fatal strain of extremism. Moderation is an English virtue. The Scots have ever been extremists: extremist feudal nobles, extremist religious zealots of all classes (and nowadays, extremist followers of mammon). In all this, the national interest has ever been passed over.

To name Wallace as a Patriot is to name a unique individual. Where were the others? Self-interest and self-promotion have been, and remain, the cause of Scotland's downfall. Scotland was a nation despite itself, when Kings like James IV, James V and James VI made it – struggling and kicking – into one.

Could it be again? Or, rather, could the Scots ever make a real go of it? Certainly not by the normal political process: the history of modern Nationalist politics has been an absurd caricature of the national failing for pointless bickering.

* * *

To research and write a History of Scotland – however sketchy – is to be a man of sorrows and acquainted with grief. It also entitles the writer, surely, to some brief conclusions of his own.

Scotland as a country undoubtedly possesses the essential quality, the character and the history of nationhood, but Scotland's people unfortunately do not. Since 1746, there have been many individual Scots who have made good, but there have been no national leaders, and such as might have been, like Ramsay MacDonald, have, as ever, been prepared to give up their principles to preserve their self-advancement.

The Scots today are at an all-time low, their popular culture a tartan joke and their economy and politics a puppet show worked by foreigners and cynics for small profits and quick returns. Yet the land exists, a land of infinite variety and spiritual power, waiting for a people to match it, to master it, to be at one with it – not just to exploit it, betray it and sing maudlin songs about it. If Finland, Norway, Faeroe and Iceland can be nations, there is only one reason why Scotland cannot be one: her own people.